WeightWatchers®

COOK SMART family food

Great-tasting recipes all the family will love,
all updated with *ProPoints*® values

SIMON &
SCHUSTER
ILLUSTRATED

London · New York · Sydney · Toronto

A CBS COMPANY

First published in Great Britain by Simon & Schuster UK Ltd, 2009
This edition published 2011
A CBS Company

Weight Watchers Publications Team: Jane Griffiths, Donna Watts, Nina McKerlie, Imogen Prescott and Cheryl Jackson.

Recipes written by Sue Ashworth, Sue Beveridge, Tamsin Burnett-Hall, Cas Clarke, Siân Davies, Roz Denny, Becky Johnson, Joy Skipper, Penny Stephens and Wendy Veale, as well as Weight Watchers Leaders and Members.

Photography by Steve Baxter, Iain Bagwell and Steve Lee.
Design and typesetting by Jane Norman and Tiger Media Ltd.
Colour reproduction by Dot Gradations Ltd, UK.
Printed and bound in China.

A CIP catalogue for this book is available from the British Library.

ISBN 978-0-85720-632-9

1 3 5 7 9 10 8 6 4 2

Pictured on the front cover: Individual Roasted Vegetable Pizzas page 50, Overnight Muesli page 24,
Roast Chicken with Rosemary and Lemon Potatoes page 72, Summer Puddings page 148.
Pictured on the introduction: Full English Breakfast, page 10, Seafood Chowder page 38, Prawn and Chilli Tagliatelle page 78,
Lemon and Ginger Tart page 144.

 ProPoints® value logo: You'll find this easy to read **ProPoints** value logo on every recipe throughout this book. The logo represents the number of **ProPoints** values per serving each recipe contains. It is not an indication of the fillingness of a recipe.

Weight Watchers **ProPoints** Weight Loss System is a simple way to lose weight. As part of the Weight Watchers **ProPoints** plan you'll enjoy eating delicious, healthy, filling foods that help to keep you feeling satisfied for longer and in control of your portions.

V This symbol denotes a vegetarian recipe and assumes that, where relevant, free range eggs, vegetarian cheese, vegetarian virtually fat free fromage frais, vegetarian low fat crème fraîche and vegetarian low fat yogurts are used. Virtually fat free fromage frais, low fat crème fraîche and low fat yogurts may contain traces of gelatine so they are not always vegetarian. Please check the labels.

✱ This symbol denotes a dish that can be frozen. Unless otherwise stated, you can freeze the finished dish for up to 3 months. Defrost thoroughly and reheat until the dish is piping hot throughout.

Recipe notes
Egg size: Medium, unless otherwise stated.
Raw eggs: Only the freshest eggs should be used. Pregnant women, the elderly and children should avoid recipes with eggs that are not fully cooked or raw.
All fruits and vegetables: Medium sized, unless otherwise stated.
Stock: Stock cubes used in recipes, unless otherwise stated. These should be prepared according to packet instructions.
Recipe timings: These are approximate and meant to be guidelines. Please note that the preparation time includes all the steps up to and following the main cooking time(s).
Microwaves: Timings and temperatures are for a standard 800 W microwave. If necessary, adjust to your own microwave.
Low fat spread: Where a recipe states to use a low fat spread, a light spread with a fat content of no less than 38% should be used.
Low fat soft cheese: Where low fat soft cheese is specified in a recipe, this refers to soft cheese with a fat content of less than 5%, such as Philadelphia Extra Light.

Contents

Introduction

This book is designed for those who want to eat healthily and make sure that their family enjoys good food. It's for people who lead busy lives and don't have a great deal of time to spend in the kitchen, but who do want to eat nutritious tasty meals every day.

As well as delicious recipes, you will find hints and tips throughout the book. Boxes on Eating Wisely, Cooking Basics and Store Cupboard Ideas should all help you to make the most of your time and provide great meals for the family.

There's extra information in the next two pages as well: tips on basic ingredients, as well as a list of useful things to keep in your store cupboard.

About Weight Watchers

For more than 40 years Weight Watchers has been helping people around the world to lose weight using a long term sustainable approach. Weight Watchers successful weight loss system is based on four tried and trusted principles:

- Eating healthily
- Being more active
- Adjusting behaviour to help weight loss
- Getting support in weekly meetings

Our unique *ProPoints* system empowers you to manage your food plan and make wise recipe choices for a healthier, happier you.

Basic Ingredients

Milk

Always use skimmed milk, rather than whole or semi skimmed, unless otherwise stated in the recipe.

Eggs

Use medium size eggs, unless otherwise stated in the recipe. Always bring eggs to room temperature before using. A cold egg won't whisk well and the shell will crack if placed in hot water.

Fats and oils

The majority of recipes use calorie controlled cooking spray rather than oil. Calorie controlled cooking spray can be either olive oil or sunflower oil based. Try both and see which you prefer.

Generally, low fat spread is used in recipes rather than butter.

Cheese and yogurt

The cheese used in these recipes is low fat Cheddar, low fat soft cheese or virtually fat free fromage frais. Many recipes use yogurt. Always choose either 0% fat Greek yogurt or low fat natural or fruit yogurt. Quark – a very low fat soft cheese made with skimmed milk – is also used. Low fat soft cheese should have a fat content of less than 50%. All of these products are easy to find in a supermarket.

Fruit and vegetables

Make sure your family eats plenty of fruit and vegetables, preferably at least five portions a day. Try putting a fruit snack in lunchboxes and always offer your family at least one vegetable with the main meal. Filling up on fruit and vegetables will also stop you from feeling hungry, so you are less likely to snack on fatty and sugary foods.

There are plenty of vegetarian recipes in the book, including healthy salads and soups, as well as suggestions for vegetable accompaniments.

Planning Ahead

When you're going around the supermarket it is tempting to pick up foods you like and put them in your trolley without thinking about how you will use them. So, a good plan is to decide what dishes you want to cook before you go shopping, check your store cupboard ingredients and make a list of what you need. You'll save time by not drifting aimlessly around the supermarket picking up what you fancy. You might even have time for a cup of tea or coffee.

Store Cupboard Suggestions

artificial sweetener
baking powder
bay leaves
bicarbonate of soda
black pepper
borlotti beans, canned
calorie controlled cooking spray
cannellini beans, canned
cereal (bran and muesli)
chick peas, canned
chilli (flakes and powder)
chocolate (minimum 70% cocoa solids)
cloves
cocoa powder
coffee, instant
condensed milk, light
cornflour
corn oil
couscous
curry powder
custard, low fat
flour (plain, brown, wholemeal and self raising)
fish sauce, Thai
fruit, canned
fruit, dried (sultanas, apricots, blueberries, etc.)
gelatine
gravy granules
herbs, dried (mixed, oregano, thyme, etc.)
honey
jam, reduced sugar
kidney beans

lentils, canned
low fat peanut butter
mayonnaise, extra light
marmalade, reduced sugar
mushrooms, dried
mustard (English and wholegrain)
noodles (rice and egg)
nuts
oil (olive and sunflower)
passata
pasta
pastry, filo
peppercorns
pizza bases
polenta (cornmeal)
porridge oats
rice (basmati, brown and risotto)
salt (sea salt or low sodium)
seeds (caraway, fennel, pumpkin and sesame)
semolina
spices, ground (cinnamon, nutmeg, ginger, paprika,
  cayenne pepper, coriander, cumin, etc.)
soy sauce, light
stock cubes (vegetable, chicken and beef)
sugar (caster, icing, demerara and muscovado)
sugar free jelly
sweetcorn, canned or frozen
tomato ketchup
tomato purée
tomatoes, canned
tuna, canned in brine or in spring water
vanilla essence
vinegar (balsamic, rice and white wine)

Breakfasts
and Brunches

Probably the most important meal of the day, breakfast can be anything from a Bold Berry Smoothie to a Big Fruit Breakfast. Or try a more leisurely weekend affair such as Eggs Florentine or Kedgeree. Choose from a wide range of healthy options that will set you up for the day and will also give the whole family an energy boost.

Start the day the right way with a
healthy breakfast

Full English Breakfast

This recipe shows you how easy it is to enjoy a full English breakfast while you are trying to lose weight.

Serves 4

200 g (7 oz) turkey rashers
4 ripe tomatoes, sliced in half crossways
4 medium slices wholemeal bread
calorie controlled cooking spray
200 g (7 oz) mushrooms, sliced
2 large lemon wedges
4 eggs
30 g (1¼ oz) low fat spread
salt and freshly ground black pepper

6 *ProPoints* values per serving
25 *ProPoints* values per recipe

240 calories per serving

Takes **20 minutes**

not recommended

1 Preheat the grill and place the turkey rashers and tomatoes, cut side up, on the grill pan. Season the tomatoes. Grill for 3–4 minutes then turn the turkey rashers over and grill again for 2 minutes, until golden and crispy.

2 Meanwhile, warm four serving plates, toast the bread and heat a non stick frying pan. Spray with the cooking spray and then add the mushrooms. Stir fry for 3–4 minutes on a high heat until softened, then season, squeeze over the lemon and remove from the heat.

3 Tip the mushrooms on to the serving plates and keep warm. Return the frying pan to a low heat. Spray again with the cooking spray and then carefully break in the eggs. Fry over a gentle heat until they are cooked how you like them.

4 Meanwhile, spread the toast with the low fat spread and slice in half, then place on the serving plates with the mushrooms. Add the cooked turkey rashers, tomatoes and eggs and serve immediately.

Eat wisely Calorie controlled cooking spray is an absolute must for eating the Weight Watchers way. It works as a substitute for oil. You can use it for frying, roasting, browning and grilling. You can get different varieties, with either sunflower or olive oil bases, depending on your preference.

Eggs Florentine

A classic brunch dish that's been adapted here for a healthier lifestyle.

Serves 4

350 g (12 oz) baby spinach leaves, washed
a couple of pinches of fresh nutmeg
1 tablespoon vinegar (any type)
4 eggs
2 muffins, sliced in half
4 tablespoons virtually fat free fromage frais
4 pinches of paprika
salt and freshly ground black pepper

---

5 *ProPoints* values per serving
21 *ProPoints* values per recipe

189 calories per serving

Takes **10 minutes**

V

* not recommended

1 Place the wet spinach in a lidded saucepan with seasoning and the nutmeg. Cover and cook on a low heat, stirring occasionally, for 3–4 minutes until wilted. Keep warm.

2 Heat a medium saucepan of water to a rolling boil and add the vinegar. One at a time, break the eggs into a cup and gently lower them from the cup into the boiling water. Poach the eggs for 2–3 minutes until the white is firm, but the yolk still runny (or how you prefer). Remove with a slotted spoon.

3 Meanwhile, toast the muffins and place on plates with a pile of the cooked spinach on each one. Make a slight hollow in the top of the spinach and carefully spoon in the poached eggs. Spoon the fromage frais over the eggs and dust with paprika to serve.

Eat wisely Opt for healthy cooking methods such as steaming, grilling or poaching rather than frying. The flavour will be just as good, but you won't need to use lots of oil or butter and any excess fat will drain away.

Bacon and Egg Bubble and Squeak

If you've got leftover vegetables, don't throw them out. They're easily added to soup or, even better, they can be made into this quick and tasty breakfast treat.

Serves 4

350 g (12 oz) cooked boiled potatoes, chopped roughly
200 g (7 oz) cooked cabbage, shredded
200 g (7 oz) cooked carrots, chopped
50 g (1¾ oz) spring onions, chopped finely
4 tablespoons chopped fresh parsley
4 eggs, beaten
2 tablespoons skimmed milk
calorie controlled cooking spray
100 g (3½ oz) lean bacon rashers, preferably smoked, snipped into small pieces
salt and freshly ground black pepper

5 *ProPoints* values per serving
18 *ProPoints* values per recipe

231 calories per serving

Takes 35 minutes

* not recommended

1 Put the potatoes, cabbage and carrots into a bowl and mix together. Stir in the spring onions, some seasoning and all but 1 tablespoon of the parsley.

2 In a separate bowl, mix the eggs with the milk and season. Set aside.

3 Spray a non stick frying pan with the cooking spray and heat to medium hot. Fry the bacon pieces for 2–3 minutes or until cooked, and then add them to the potato mixture. Turn the heat down to medium and remove the pan from the hob.

4 Use your hands to squeeze the mixture together and form eight balls. Spray the pan with a little more cooking spray and put the balls in the frying pan. Gently squash down on them to make little patty shapes and return the pan to the heat. Fry them for 5 minutes on each side or until they are brown and heated right through. You may have to do this in batches. Remove them and put two patties on each plate.

5 Reduce the temperature of the pan, spray it again with the cooking spray and pour the eggs into the frying pan, stirring continuously. The eggs will cook in seconds, so be ready to remove the pan from the heat and top the patties with the eggs. Garnish with the remaining parsley and serve immediately.

Vegetarian variation Omit the bacon for a vegetarian bubble and squeak, reducing the *ProPoints* values to 4 per serving.

Potato Pancakes with Turkey Rashers and Tomatoes

A tempting treat for a weekend brunch, these potato pancakes are also a healthy alternative to hash browns.

Serves 4

2 eggs, beaten
30 g (1¼ oz) self raising flour
450 g (1 lb) baking potatoes, peeled
calorie controlled cooking spray
8 turkey rashers
4 tomatoes, halved
salt and freshly ground black pepper

5 ProPoints values per serving
21 ProPoints values per recipe

221 calories per serving

Takes **20 minutes**

＊ not recommended

1 Preheat the grill. Mix the eggs and flour together to form a batter.

2 Coarsely grate the potatoes then squeeze out the excess moisture. Stir into the batter and season generously.

3 Lightly coat a lidded non stick frying pan with the cooking spray then spoon half the potato mixture into the pan as four separate pancakes. Cook over a medium heat for 3 minutes each side until golden brown.

4 Reduce the heat, cover the pan and cook for 2 minutes more to cook the pancakes through. Remove and keep warm. Repeat with the other half of the potato mixture.

5 Meanwhile, grill the turkey rashers and tomatoes for about 5 minutes, or until cooked to your liking. Serve with the potato pancakes.

Store cupboard ideas Always keep some pepper in the cupboard as it adds a final, distinctive flavour to your dishes. You can buy pepper whole, cracked or ground – but try to buy whole peppercorns and then pop them in a pepper mill for freshly ground pepper any time. Freshly ground pepper is more pungent than pre-ground and can be stored for up to a year.

Sweetcorn Fritters

This cooked breakfast is a taste of America – a delicious, different way to start the day.

Serves 4

calorie controlled cooking spray
4 eggs, beaten
½ red onion, diced finely
½ teaspoon mustard powder (optional)
200 g (7 oz) sweetcorn
2 tablespoons chopped fresh parsley or
** coriander, plus extra to garnish**
2 beef tomatoes, each sliced into at least
** four slices**
salt and freshly ground black pepper

4 *ProPoints* values per serving
14 *ProPoints* values per recipe

166 calories per serving

Takes **20 minutes**

V

✱ not recommended

1 Spray a large non stick frying pan or griddle pan with the cooking spray and preheat to a medium hot temperature.

2 Using a fork or a balloon whisk, combine all the ingredients except the tomato slices in a large mixing bowl. Season well. Create a fritter by putting two generous tablespoons of the mixture into the pan. (Stir the mix between each spoonful, or the corn will all sink to the bottom of the bowl). If all the corn is in the middle of the fritter, gently spread the kernels out to its edges.

3 Repeat with another two spoonfuls of mixture at the other side of the pan and cook both fritters for a minute or two, or until the egg has set enough to turn the fritters over. Cook on the other side for a couple of minutes and check both sides are browned. While the fritters are cooking, pop the tomato slices into the pan and heat through on both sides.

4 Cook the fritters in batches, keeping them warm until you have eight cooked fritters. Warm four plates. Serve each fritter topped with a slice of tomato and a sprinkling of fresh herbs.

Kedgeree

This makes an excellent weekend breakfast for the whole family.

Serves 4

200 g (7 oz) dried long grain rice
2 tablespoons medium curry powder
2 eggs
400 g (14 oz) smoked haddock fillets
300 ml (10 fl oz) fish or vegetable stock
calorie controlled cooking spray
1 onion, chopped
2 tablespoons chopped fresh parsley
2 tomatoes, each cut into six wedges
salt and freshly ground black pepper

9 *ProPoints* values per serving
35 *ProPoints* values per recipe

335 calories per serving

Takes **25 minutes**

* not recommended

1 Put the rice and curry powder in a lidded pan and cover with water. Bring to the boil, cover and simmer for 10 minutes.

2 Meanwhile, hard boil the eggs in simmering water for 8 minutes (see Cooking basics, below).

3 Place the haddock and stock in a large lidded frying pan, cover and cook for 6 minutes (until the fish flakes easily).

4 Spray a non stick frying pan with the cooking spray and cook the onion until just starting to brown.

5 When the fish is cooked, skin and flake the flesh.

6 When the eggs are cooked, plunge into cold water to cool and then remove the shells. Cut into wedges.

7 When the rice is cooked, drain if necessary and then stir in 1 tablespoon of chopped parsley, the onion and fish. Season to taste.

8 Divide the kedgeree between four warmed serving plates, garnish with wedges of egg and tomato and sprinkle with the remaining parsley. Serve immediately.

Cooking basics For perfect hard boiled eggs: try to always use an egg that is at room temperature, rather than one straight from the fridge. Place the eggs in a small saucepan and add enough cold water to just cover them. Slowly bring the water to simmering point and let the eggs cook for about 8 minutes. Gently take the eggs out of the pan and run cold water over them before allowing them to rest in cold water for a couple of minutes.

Smoked Salmon and Scrambled Eggs

6 ProPoints value

A satisfying start to the day with a luxurious twist. Fresh dill or parsley makes a delicious addition.

Serves 2

4 eggs, beaten
8 tablespoons skimmed milk or soya milk
**100 g (3½ oz) smoked salmon pieces,
  chopped if necessary**
calorie controlled cooking spray
salt and freshly ground black pepper

1 In a large bowl, mix all the ingredients except the cooking spray together.

2 Spray a non stick frying pan with the cooking spray and place over a low heat. Pour the mixture into the frying pan and, using a wooden spoon, stir until the eggs are just firm but not dry.

3 Season to taste and serve immediately.

6 ProPoints values per serving
12 ProPoints values per recipe

273 calories per serving

Takes **5 minutes**

not recommended

Tip You can usually buy smoked salmon offcuts quite cheaply in supermarkets and they are perfect for this recipe, which requires the salmon to be chopped into small pieces.

Breakfast Omelette

Save on the washing up with this one pan version of a cooked breakfast.

Serves 1

calorie controlled cooking spray
80 g (3 oz) button mushrooms, quartered
5 cherry tomatoes, halved
2 eggs
salt and freshly ground black pepper

1 Lightly coat a large non stick frying pan with the cooking spray and cook the mushrooms for 2 minutes, then add the tomatoes.

2 Beat the eggs with 4 tablespoons of water and seasoning, then pour into the pan. Tip the pan from side to side to spread the egg around, then cook gently for 3–4 minutes, or until set to your liking. Carefully fold over and serve on a warmed plate.

4 ProPoints values per serving
4 ProPoints values per recipe

C **196 calories** per serving

Takes **10 minutes**

V

* not recommended

Cinnamon French Toast with Apricots

A sweet version of eggy bread that's wonderful for a lazy weekend breakfast.

Serves 4

1 teaspoon ground cinnamon
4 teaspoons artificial sweetener
4 eggs
4 tablespoons skimmed milk
6 medium slices wholemeal bread
calorie controlled cooking spray

To serve

2 x 410 g cans apricot halves in natural juice, drained
4 heaped tablespoons very low fat plain fromage frais

6 ProPoints values per serving
23 ProPoints values per recipe

C **246 calories** per serving

Takes **10 minutes**

V

✳ not recommended

1 Mix half the cinnamon with the sweetener and set aside.

2 Beat the remaining cinnamon together with the eggs and milk in a shallow dish. Cut the bread into triangles and dip into the egg mixture.

3 Lightly coat a non stick frying pan with the cooking spray. Cook the eggy bread in four batches, frying over a medium heat for 1½–2 minutes on each side until golden and crisp. Keep warm while you cook the other batches.

4 Divide the French toast between four plates and sprinkle with the cinnamon sugar. Top with the apricots and fromage frais and serve immediately.

Eat wisely If bread is your downfall, an easy way to control what you eat is by freezing your sliced bread. When you are hungry or want some toast, either pop a couple of frozen slices straight into the toaster (for slightly longer than from fresh) or allow the bread to thaw before eating.

Overnight Muesli

Oats make for a great breakfast as they provide slow-release energy throughout the morning.

Serves 2

60 g (2 oz) porridge oats
1 apple, cored and grated coarsely
250 ml (9 fl oz) skimmed milk

To serve
2 heaped tablespoons 0% fat Greek yogurt
80 g (3 oz) fresh blueberries

---

5 ProPoints values per serving
9 ProPoints values per recipe

200 calories per serving

Takes **5 minutes** + overnight soaking

V

✳ not recommended

1 Place the oats in a bowl or plastic container, stir in the apple and milk, cover and leave to soak and soften overnight in the fridge.

2 In the morning, top each bowlful with a heaped tablespoon of yogurt and the blueberries.

Store cupboard ideas Replace highly processed breakfast cereals with wholegrain, unsweetened varieties, but better still faze them out and make your own. Vary your breakfast with fruit, porridge oats, eggs and smoothies.

Oaty Pancakes with Blueberries

These delicious cinnamon-flavoured fluffy pancakes make a very special breakfast or delectable dessert.

Serves 4

2 eggs, separated
50 g (1¾ oz) self raising flour
50 g (1¾ oz) porridge oats
1 tablespoon artificial sweetener, plus an extra pinch
1 teaspoon ground cinnamon
150 ml (5 fl oz) skimmed milk or soya milk
calorie controlled cooking spray
150 g (5½ oz) fresh blueberries

---

4 *ProPoints* values per serving
14 *ProPoints* values per recipe

C **170 calories** per serving

Takes **20 minutes**

V

✳ not recommended

1 Whisk the egg whites in a clean, grease-free bowl until stiff. In another large bowl beat together the egg yolks, flour, oats, the pinch of sweetener, cinnamon and milk.

2 Fold the egg whites into the mixture with a large metal spoon, being careful to preserve as much of the volume as possible.

3 Heat a non stick frying pan and spray with the cooking spray. Place tablespoons of the batter in the frying pan to make little oval pancakes approximately 8 cm (3¼ inches) in diameter.

4 Cook for 2–3 minutes until golden and spongy and then turn once, using a palette knife or fish slice, and cook until golden on the other side.

5 When cooked, place them on a plate and wrap in a clean tea towel. Keep warm while you cook the others (the mixture makes 16 pancakes).

6 Meanwhile warm the blueberries gently in a small saucepan with 100 ml (3½ fl oz) of water and the tablespoon of sweetener. Stir occasionally until the fruit has broken down.

7 Serve the pancakes warm with the hot blueberry sauce, allowing four pancakes per person.

Banana and Honey Crumpets

Popular with adults and children alike, these crumpets are terrific for breakfast or an after work snack.

Serves 4

8 regular crumpets
60 g (2 oz) low fat soft cheese
2 bananas, sliced
¼ teaspoon mixed spice or cinnamon
2 heaped teaspoons honey

6 *ProPoints* values per serving
24 *ProPoints* values per recipe

260 calories per serving

Takes **5 minutes**

V

✳ not recommended

1 Preheat the grill. Toast the crumpets under the grill then spread with the soft cheese. Pile the banana slices on top, sprinkle with mixed spice or cinnamon and return to the grill for 1 minute to warm through.

2 Drizzle with the honey and eat straightaway.

Eat wisely Replace cream cheese with low fat soft cheeses. However, always check the pack carefully to make sure that it says low fat soft cheese and not medium fat soft cheese, as sometimes the labelling can be deceptive.

Blueberry Muffins

This recipe can be made using dried blueberries, which can be found in the baking section of supermarkets. These are very convenient to keep in your store cupboard.

Makes 12

200 g (7 oz) plain flour
½ teaspoon bicarbonate of soda
2 teaspoons baking powder
75 g (2¾ oz) caster sugar
a pinch of salt
75 g (2¾ oz) low fat spread, melted
100 ml (3½ fl oz) low fat natural yogurt
100 ml (3½ fl oz) skimmed milk
1 egg
200 g (7 oz) fresh blueberries

3 *ProPoints* values per serving
40 *ProPoints* values per recipe

C **125 calories** per muffin

Takes **15 minutes** to prepare,
20 minutes to bake

V

✱ not recommended

1 Preheat the oven to Gas Mark 6/200°C/fan oven 180°C. Line a Yorkshire pudding tin or muffin tray with 12 muffin or cup cake cases.

2 Combine all the dry ingredients in a bowl. In another bowl mix the melted low fat spread, yogurt, milk and egg together.

3 Pour the wet ingredients into the dry and combine very gently so you don't overwork the mixture.

4 Gently stir in the blueberries, again keeping the mixing to a minimum, then quickly spoon into the muffin cases. Bake for 20 minutes, until risen and golden on top.

5 Transfer to a wire rack and cool or eat warm.

Tip These muffins keep well for up to 3 days stored in an airtight container.

Variation Substitute the fresh blueberries with 75 g (2¾ oz) of dried blueberries; just soak for 10 minutes in hot water. The *ProPoints* values per serving will be 4.

Cinnamon and Apple Muffins

These light and healthy muffins can be made in just 30 minutes. They are perfect for breakfast, especially if you are on the go.

Makes 12

1 egg
75 g (2¾ oz) low fat spread, melted
125 ml (4 fl oz) low fat natural yogurt
100 ml (3½ fl oz) apple juice
3 tablespoons clear honey, warmed
2 large dessert apples, peeled, cored and grated
200 g (7 oz) plain flour
2 teaspoons baking powder
½ teaspoon bicarbonate of soda
a pinch of salt
1 teaspoon ground cinnamon

1 Preheat the oven to Gas Mark 6/200°C/fan oven 180°C. Line a Yorkshire pudding tin or muffin tray with 12 muffin cases.

2 In a large measuring jug beat together the egg, low fat spread, yogurt, apple juice, honey and grated apple. Mix all the dry ingredients together in a large bowl. Add the wet ingredients to the dry and gently, but quickly, mix together, then spoon into the muffin cases.

3 Bake for 20 minutes or until risen and the centres spring back when gently pressed. Place on a wire rack to cool and store in an airtight container for up to 3 days.

3 *ProPoints* values per serving
38 *ProPoints* values per recipe

C **115 calories** per muffin

Takes **15 minutes** to prepare, **20 minutes** to bake + cooling

V

✱ not recommended

Tip Use dessert apples (such as Cox, Gala or Spartan) for the best results.

Bold Berry Smoothie

Smoothies can be a tasty way of helping towards the recommended five portions of fruit and vegetables in your diet every day.

Serves 2

2 small ripe bananas
300 g (10½ oz) frozen mixed summer fruits
200 g (7 oz) very low fat natural yogurt

1 Blend all the ingredients in a liquidiser, adding small quantities of water until you have the consistency you prefer. Drink immediately.

1 *ProPoints* value per serving
3 *ProPoints* values per recipe

C **193 calories** per serving

Takes **5 minutes**

V

✳ recommended

Tip Freeze the smoothie mixture in ice lolly moulds or ice cube trays for delicious, cooling summer treats.

Big Fruit Breakfast

Claimed to be the optimum breakfast, fruit is easy to digest and consequently quick to give you energy.

Serves 2

2 apples, cored and chopped
2 pears, cored and chopped
2 oranges, peeled and sliced
4 plums, stoned and chopped
2 kiwi fruit, peeled and chopped
4 heaped tablespoons low fat plain bio yogurt

1 *ProPoints* value per serving
3 *ProPoints* values per recipe

C **279 calories** per serving

Takes **10 minutes**

V

* not recommended

1 In a large bowl, toss all the fruit together. Divide equally between two bowls.

2 Spoon over the yogurt and serve immediately.

Tip Vary the fruit, try to buy whatever is ripe and in season for the best flavour. Look for local produce as the less a fruit has travelled the fresher it should be. Huge bowls of pick-your-own raspberries and strawberries in the summer are wonderful.

Eat wisely Trying out new combinations is a great way to maintain your motivation when losing weight. Relish everything that you put in your mouth and ask yourself if you're really enjoying it. Cultivate your likes, and experiment with new flavours and textures.

Hot Cross Buns

Makes 16

25 g (1 oz) fresh yeast (or 15 g/½ oz dried)
½ teaspoon caster sugar
150 ml (5 fl oz) warm water
350 g (12 oz) plain flour, plus extra for dusting
100 g (3½ oz) plain wholemeal flour
150 ml (5 fl oz) skimmed milk
1 teaspoon cinnamon
1 teaspoon ground nutmeg
1 teaspoon salt
50 g (1¾ oz) caster sugar
75 g (2¾ oz) currants
50 g (1¾ oz) chopped mixed peel
50 g (1¾ oz) low fat spread, melted
1 egg, beaten
calorie controlled cooking spray
a little skimmed milk, to glaze

1 Blend the yeast with the ½ teaspoon of sugar and a little of the warm water. Leave for 5 minutes in a warm place to froth then add the rest of the water. Meanwhile, sift half the quantity of each flour into a bowl and make a well in the centre. Pour the yeast mixture and the milk into the well in the flour. Mix well then leave, covered, in a warm place for about 45 minutes until risen to double its size.

2 Meanwhile, sieve the rest of each flour then mix with the spices, salt, caster sugar, currants and peel. Add this mixture to the risen dough with the low fat spread and egg and mix well with your hands, kneading until smooth. Leave, covered, in a warm place for 1 hour.

3 Turn the risen dough out on to a floured surface and roll or pat it out. Divide into 16 pieces. Shape them into rounds and place well apart on a baking tray that has been sprayed with the cooking spray and then lightly floured.

4 Mark each round with a cross using a sharp knife. Cover and leave either in the fridge overnight ready for baking the next day, or in a warm place for 15 minutes while you preheat the oven to Gas Mark 7/220°C/fan oven 200°C. Brush with a little milk to glaze then bake for 15 minutes. Leave on a wire rack to cool.

4 *ProPoints* values per serving
68 *ProPoints* values per recipe

C 149 calories per bun

Takes 30 minutes to prepare +
2–2½ hours rising, 15 minutes to bake

V

* recommended

Tip You can start making these the day before and keep the dough in the fridge to bake in the morning. Remember to remove it from the fridge and leave in a warm place for 30 minutes before baking.

Banana Bread

Everyone loves banana bread, and the sultanas make this version extra fruity.

Makes 12 slices

calorie controlled cooking spray
200 g (7 oz) self raising flour
¼ teaspoon bicarbonate of soda
75 g (2¾ oz) low fat spread
75 g (2¾ oz) sugar
1 tablespoon honey or an extra tablespoon sugar (optional)
2 eggs, beaten
2 ripe bananas, mashed
100 g (3½ oz) sultanas (optional)

1   Preheat the oven to Gas Mark 4/180°C/fan oven 160°C. Spray a 450 g (1 lb) loaf tin with the cooking spray.

2   In a large bowl, sieve the flour and bicarbonate of soda together. In another bowl, cream the low fat spread, sugar and honey or extra sugar, if using, until light and fluffy. Add the eggs gradually, beating all the time. Gently stir the flour into the creamed mixture, then add the mashed bananas and sultanas, if using.

3   Spoon into the prepared tin and bake for about an hour or until just firm. Turn out and cool on a rack.

4 ProPoints values per serving
47 ProPoints values per recipe

C   **159 calories** per slice

Takes **10 minutes** to prepare + cooling, **1 hour** to bake

V

*   recommended

Lunches
and Light Bites

For a delicious lunch try something simple, such as Lemony Chicken Salad, Individual Roasted Vegetable Pizzas or Spring Rolls. Or sit down to a more substantial family meal such as Beef Fillet with Horseradish Crust.

Brighten up your lunchtime
by trying something different

Seafood Chowder

Chowders are thick, chunky soups with a creamy base. They are especially popular in America.

Serves 4

calorie controlled cooking spray
1 onion, chopped finely
250 g (9 oz) potatoes, peeled and diced
850 ml (1½ pints) hot vegetable stock
50 g (1¾ oz) frozen peas
200 g (7 oz) smoked haddock, skinned,
  boned and cut into chunks
100 g (3½ oz) cooked and peeled prawns,
  defrosted if frozen
300 ml (10 fl oz) skimmed milk
2 tablespoons chopped fresh parsley
2 tablespoons cornflour
salt and freshly ground black pepper

5 *ProPoints* values per serving
22 *ProPoints* values per recipe

205 **calories** per serving

Takes **15 minutes** to prepare,
20 minutes to cook

✳ recommended

1 Lightly spray a large, lidded, non stick saucepan with the cooking spray and sauté the onion for 5 minutes, until softened.

2 Add the potatoes and stock to the saucepan. Heat, then cover and simmer gently for about 15 minutes, until the potatoes are tender.

3 Add the peas, haddock, prawns, milk and half the parsley. Cook over a low heat for about 5 minutes, until the fish is opaque.

4 Blend the cornflour with 5 tablespoons of cold water to make a paste and add to the saucepan. Heat, stirring until thickened. Season, then serve in four warmed bowls, sprinkled with the remaining parsley.

Cooking basics To skin fish: lay the fish fillet skin side down and make a small cut at the tail end, through the flesh to the skin. Place the fish with the tail towards you, then put the blade of the knife under the skin where it has been cut. Holding the skin firmly with your other hand, slide the blade away from you, up to the head of the fish, and then discard the skin.

Chicken Noodle Soup

A bowlful of this tasty low *ProPoints* value soup, with its authentic Chinese flavour, is wonderfully filling and enjoyable.

Serves 4

850 ml (1½ pints) hot chicken stock

a bunch of spring onions, shredded into fine strips

1 small leek, shredded into fine strips

½ teaspoon Chinese five spice

1 teaspoon finely grated fresh root ginger or ¼ teaspoon ground ginger

2 tablespoons light soy sauce

50 g (1¾ oz) dried thread egg noodles

50 g (1¾ oz) sweetcorn, defrosted if frozen

50 g (1¾ oz) cooked chicken breasts, shredded into fine strips

1 tablespoon cornflour

salt and freshly ground black pepper

3 *ProPoints* values per serving
13 *ProPoints* values per recipe

125 calories per serving

Takes **35 minutes**

recommended

1 Pour the chicken stock into a large lidded saucepan and add the spring onions, leek, Chinese five spice, ginger and soy sauce. Cover and cook gently for 10 minutes.

2 Add the egg noodles to the saucepan and cook gently for 5 minutes. Add the sweetcorn and chicken and cook for 2 minutes more.

3 Blend the cornflour with 3 tablespoons of cold water to make a paste. Mix into the soup and cook for about 1 minute, stirring, until the soup is thickened and smooth. Season to taste.

4 Ladle the soup into four warmed bowls and serve at once.

Variation Substitute dried long grain rice for the noodles, adding it with the soy sauce in step 1 so that it has time to cook. The *ProPoints* values will remain the same.

Leek and Potato Soup

A perfect winter soup; smooth, subtle, substantial and comforting. It is simple and quick to make and full of goodness.

Serves 4

calorie controlled cooking spray

400 g (14 oz) potatoes, peeled and chopped into small pieces

6 large leeks, split in half, washed and chopped finely

1.2 litres (2 pints) vegetable stock

300 ml (10 fl oz) skimmed milk

a pinch of nutmeg

salt and freshly ground black pepper

a bunch of chives, snipped, to garnish (optional)

3 ProPoints values per serving
13 ProPoints values per recipe

175 calories per serving

Takes **15 minutes** to prepare, **20 minutes** to cook

V

✳ recommended

1 Heat a large lidded saucepan and spray with the cooking spray. Add the potatoes and stir fry for a few minutes. Add the leeks, stir together and add the stock.

2 Bring to the boil and then simmer, covered, for 20 minutes, until the leeks and potatoes are tender.

3 Add the milk, nutmeg and seasoning and stir through. Serve hot, garnished with snipped chives, if using, and black pepper.

Cooking basics Make soups into an instant snack or lunch by preparing them in advance and freezing. Make a large batch by multiplying the recipe quantities. Then measure the soup out into portions and freeze. When you are ready to eat, simply take it out of the freezer and pop in it the microwave, or gently thaw it on the hob for a quick, wholesome and satisfying filler.

Farmhouse Chicken and Vegetable Broth

Enjoy this mighty main meal soup with the family for a Saturday lunch.

Serves 4

calorie controlled cooking spray

1 large onion, sliced finely

2 large carrots, peeled and cut into 1 cm (½ inch) slices

2 celery sticks, sliced

250 g (9 oz) swede, peeled and cut into chunks

65 g (2¼ oz) dried pearl barley

500 g (1 lb 2 oz) skinless boneless chicken thighs

1.5 litres (2¾ pints) hot chicken or vegetable stock

350 g (12 oz) mushrooms, sliced thickly

1 teaspoon dried sage (or 1 tablespoon finely chopped fresh sage)

2 tablespoons cornflour

2 teaspoons Worcestershire sauce

salt and freshly ground black pepper

2 tablespoons chopped fresh parsley, to garnish

9 *ProPoints* values per serving
37 *ProPoints* values per recipe

270 calories per serving

Takes **30 minutes** to prepare, **40 minutes** to cook

✳ recommended

1 Spray a large lidded casserole dish or saucepan with the cooking spray. Stir fry the onion, carrots, celery and swede for 5 minutes until slightly softened. Add the pearl barley and the chicken thighs. Continue to stir fry for 3–4 minutes, or until the chicken is lightly coloured.

2 Add the stock and bring to the boil, then lower the heat, cover and simmer gently for 35–40 minutes. (During this time the barley will swell and soften, absorbing some of the stock.)

3 Use tongs to remove the cooked chicken to a chopping board. Add the mushrooms and sage to the saucepan and continue to simmer, uncovered, for 10 minutes. Meanwhile, shred the chicken roughly. Return the meat to the saucepan. Season to taste.

4 Blend the cornflour to a paste with the Worcestershire sauce and a drop of cold water. Stir into the broth and continue to heat through until the broth thickens slightly. Check the seasoning.

5 Ladle into warm bowls, scatter the parsley over and serve immediately.

Tips Choose chicken thighs or legs for the best flavour and succulence.

Dark-gilled open mushrooms will add more flavour and depth to this broth than button mushrooms, so look out for them.

Avocado, Tomato and Cucumber Salad

This refreshing salad is delicious and makes a perfect lunch.

Serves 4

12 Cos or Romaine lettuce leaves
225 g (8 oz) tomatoes, chopped
1 small avocado, peeled and diced
½ cucumber, diced
2 tablespoons olive oil
½ teaspoon finely grated lemon zest
2 tablespoons lemon juice
1 small garlic clove, crushed
2 teaspoons Dijon mustard
salt and freshly ground black pepper
2–3 tablespoons chopped fresh coriander,
  mint or basil (or all three), to garnish

4 *ProPoints* values per serving
17 *ProPoints* values per recipe

140 calories per serving

Takes **10 minutes**

V

*   not recommended

1   Arrange three lettuce leaves on each of four serving plates.

2   Mix together the tomatoes, avocado and cucumber and pile into the lettuce leaves.

3   Make the dressing by mixing together the olive oil, lemon zest and juice, garlic and mustard. Season to taste.

4   Spoon the dressing over the salads and serve at once, scattered with the herbs.

Tips Use a mixture of tomatoes for a variety of flavours – Sungold, cherry and vine tomatoes taste delicious together.

Store cupboard ideas Herbs are always good to have to hand. You can add so much flavour, without any fat, by simply adding a sprinkling of herbs to your dishes. Experiment until you find your favourite varieties, and then always try to keep some handy. You can buy dried or fresh herbs from all the supermarkets – and if you are really ambitious you can even try growing your own.

Sweet Potato and Sausage Salad

Roasted sweet potatoes are delicious eaten hot or cold and make a great salad ingredient, especially when combined with sausage and a creamy mustard dressing.

Serves 4

600 g (1 lb 5 oz) sweet potatoes
calorie controlled cooking spray
8 thin reduced fat sausages
4 shallots, chopped finely
a small bunch of fresh chives, chopped
salt and freshly ground black pepper

For the dressing
4 tablespoons half fat crème fraîche
1 tablespoon Dijon mustard

8 ProPoints values per serving
32 ProPoints values per recipe

190 calories per serving

Takes **15 minutes** to prepare + cooling,
30 minutes to cook

* not recommended

1 Preheat the oven to Gas Mark 7/220°C/fan oven 200°C. Scrub the potatoes and cut into wedges. Place in a roasting tin, spray with the cooking spray, season then roast for 30 minutes until tender.

2 Meanwhile, preheat the grill and line the grill pan with foil. Grill the sausages for about 5 minutes on each side until browned and cooked through. Leave to cool, then chop into pieces.

3 Heat a non stick frying pan, spray with the cooking spray and stir fry the shallots for 5 minutes until softened, adding a little water to stop them from sticking if necessary.

4 Place the sweet potato, sausages, shallots and chives in a bowl. In a separate bowl stir together the dressing ingredients, then spoon over the potatoes. Toss the salad together and serve.

Variation Use ordinary potatoes instead of sweet potatoes. The **ProPoints** values per serving will be 7.

Cook's note As an alternative to roasting, put the sweet potatoes into a large pan of boiling water or stock for 10–12 minutes.

Lemony Chicken Salad

This is a very quick and refreshing lunch salad – or you could divide it into six portions for a starter, each with a *ProPoints* value of 6 per serving.

Serves 4

150 g (5½ oz) dried fusilli bucati (short spirals)
500 g (1 lb 2 oz) cooked chicken breasts, shredded into strips
10 cm (4 inches) cucumber, diced
4 spring onions, chopped
16 cherry tomatoes, halved
8 tablespoons fat free dressing
2 tablespoons fresh tarragon, chopped
finely grated zest of a lemon
salt and freshly ground black pepper

9 *ProPoints* values per serving
34 *ProPoints* values per recipe

334 calories per serving

Takes **20 minutes** + **30 minutes** chilling (optional)

＊ not recommended

1 Bring a large pan of water to the boil, add the pasta and cook for 10–12 minutes or according to the packet instructions. Drain and rinse in plenty of cold water. Drain again.

2 Toss in the rest of the ingredients and mix to combine. Season to taste.

Tip Chill the salad for 30 minutes before serving to allow the flavours to develop.

Variation Serve the salad with torn Cos lettuce leaves for extra crunch.

Eat wisely Always try to make your own lunches – it doesn't have to be laborious. Shop bought lunches (whether it's a sandwich or a salad) can be deceptively high in fat. Making your own not only means that you will be able to control what you are eating more effectively, but you'll also save money.

Turkey Ciabatta Grills

Turkey rashers make a tasty topping for these grilled open sandwiches.

Serves 4

300 g (10½ oz) ciabatta loaf with sun-dried
  tomatoes or olives
2 tablespoons sun-dried tomato purée
150 g (5½ oz) grilled red and yellow
  pepper strips (see Tip)
8 turkey rashers, uncooked
salt and freshly ground black pepper
a few basil leaves, to garnish

9 *ProPoints* values per serving
35 *ProPoints* values per recipe

225 calories per serving

Takes **10 minutes**

not recommended

1 Preheat the grill to high.

2 Slice the loaf in half lengthways and spread with the tomato purée.

3 Top both pieces of ciabatta with the pepper strips, then the uncooked turkey rashers. Grill for 1½ minutes, then turn the rashers over and grill for another 1½ minutes, until the rashers are cooked.

4 Slice each piece of bread in half, season to taste and scatter with a few basil leaves. Serve immediately.

Tip Look for grilled pepper strips in jars, preserved in vinegar, then rinse and drain them. Alternatively, you can buy canned red peppers (sometimes called pimientos) which simply need to be drained and sliced.

Pitta Pockets with Roasted Vegetables

Serves 4

250 g (9 oz) courgettes, cut into chunks
2 red onions, cut into wedges
1 aubergine, cubed
2 small green peppers, de-seeded and diced
2 tablespoons balsamic vinegar
calorie controlled cooking spray
200 g (7 oz) cherry tomatoes, halved
150 g (5½ oz) low fat soft cheese with garlic and herbs, cubed
4 pitta breads
salt and freshly ground black pepper

5 _ProPoints_ values per serving
21 _ProPoints_ values per recipe

264 calories per serving

Takes **15 minutes** to prepare,
30 minutes to cook

V

＊ not recommended

1 Preheat the oven to Gas Mark 5/190°C/fan oven 170°C. Line a roasting tin with non stick baking parchment.

2 In a large bowl, mix together the courgettes, onions, aubergine, green peppers, balsamic vinegar and seasoning. Spray with a little cooking spray.

3 Arrange the vegetables in the roasting tin and cook for 25 minutes, turning them halfway through. Remove from the oven and mix in the tomatoes and cheese. Return to the oven for 5 minutes.

4 Warm the pitta breads in the oven for the last 5 minutes of the roasting time.

5 Split the warm pittas lengthways, pile the cooked mixture into the middle and serve.

Tip Balsamic vinegar can be quite expensive – choose the best you can afford as a little goes a long way. Its sweet, sticky flavour is quite different to ordinary vinegar.

Individual Roasted Vegetable Pizzas

These pizzas are great to eat at lunchtime with friends as they are heaped with delicious roasted vegetables and are very substantial.

Serves 4

1 butternut squash, peeled de-seeded and
  cut into chunks
1 red onion, cut into wedges
8 baby carrots, scrubbed and tops trimmed
1 red pepper, de-seeded and diced
3 sprigs of rosemary
calorie controlled cooking spray
144 g packet pizza base mix
4 teaspoons olive oil
1 garlic clove, crushed
12 cherry tomatoes
salt and freshly ground black pepper

4 *ProPoints* values per serving
17 *ProPoints* values per recipe

270 calories per serving

Takes **25 minutes** to prepare +
10 minutes proving, **50 minutes** to cook

V

*   not recommended

1 Preheat the oven to Gas Mark 6/ 200°C/fan oven 180°C. Place the squash, onion, carrots and pepper, with two sprigs of rosemary, in a large roasting tin, spray with the cooking spray and toss so that they are evenly coated. Roast for 40 minutes, turning occasionally, until the vegetables are tender and beginning to char. Remove from the oven and discard the sticks from the rosemary, leaving any loose leaves. Increase the oven temperature to Gas Mark 7/220°C/fan oven 200°C.

2 Meanwhile, make up the pizza base according to the packet instructions. Divide the dough into four and knead to make 12 cm (4½ inch) rounds. Place on a baking tray sprayed with the cooking spray and leave to rise for 10 minutes.

3 Remove the leaves from the remaining rosemary sprig and chop finely. Mix with the olive oil and garlic and season.

4 Top the pizza bases with the roasted vegetables and cherry tomatoes and drizzle over the oil. Bake for 12–15 minutes until golden. Serve hot or cold.

Tip You could cook the vegetables up to 24 hours in advance, then cover and chill until required.

Falafel with Cucumber and Mint Dressing

Serves 4

calorie controlled cooking spray
1 small onion, chopped finely
1 garlic clove, crushed
1 teaspoon ground coriander
1 teaspoon ground cumin
½ teaspoon chilli flakes
425 g (15 oz) can chick peas, drained and rinsed
1 egg
25 g (1 oz) wholemeal breadcrumbs
3 tablespoons chopped fresh coriander
salt and freshly ground black pepper
shredded lettuce, to serve

For the dressing
150 ml (5 fl oz) low fat natural yogurt
2 tablespoons mint jelly
175 g (6 oz) cucumber, diced finely

4 *ProPoints* values per serving
15 *ProPoints* values per recipe

162 calories per serving

Takes **25 minutes** to prepare,
20 minutes to cook

V

✱ recommended (falafel only)

1 Preheat the oven to Gas Mark 5/190°C/fan oven 170°C. Heat a non stick frying pan and spray with the cooking spray. Gently cook the onion and garlic until softened but not browned. Stir in the coriander, cumin and chilli flakes. Cook for 1 minute and then remove from the heat.

2 Place the onion mixture in a food processor with the chick peas, egg, breadcrumbs, seasoning and fresh coriander.Blend until evenly combined and then, using clean hands, shape the mixture into about 20 small balls.

3 Arrange the falafel on a non stick baking tray and cook for 20 minutes.

4 To make the dressing, mix together the yogurt and mint jelly. Stir in the cucumber. Season to taste.

5 Serve the cooked falafel on a bed of shredded lettuce, drizzled with the mint and cucumber dressing.

Cooking basics To slice an onion finely: if you don't have a food processor, but need to slice onions finely, peel off the skin but don't cut off the root at the bottom. Slice the onion in half then slice it from the top, but don't cut through the root as this holds the onion together. Now slice horizontally across the vertical cuts. Finally, chop off the roots and discard. You should have very finely sliced onion.

Thai Fish Cakes

Crab cakes are a Thai speciality – and no wonder, as they taste so good. Serve them with a zero *ProPoints* value vegetable stir fry or salad.

Serves 4

2 teaspoons sesame oil
75 g (2¾ oz) dried long grain rice
3 shallots or 1 small onion, chopped
1 large garlic clove, crushed
2 tablespoons chopped fresh coriander
170 g can crabmeat, drained
1 tablespoon Thai fish sauce or light
  soy sauce
200 ml (7 fl oz) reduced fat coconut milk
2 eggs, beaten
2 teaspoons Thai red curry paste
salt and freshly ground black pepper
spring onions, red chillies and sprigs of
  fresh coriander, to garnish

6 *ProPoints* values per serving
22 *ProPoints* values per recipe

225 calories per serving

Takes **20 minutes** to prepare,
25–30 minutes to cook

✻ recommended

1 Preheat the oven to Gas Mark 4/180°C/fan oven 160°C. Grease four 200 ml (7 fl oz) ramekins with ½ teaspoon of the oil.

2 Bring a pan of water to the boil, add the rice and cook for about 12 minutes, until just tender. Rinse with cold water and drain well.

3 Heat the remaining oil in a small non stick frying pan and sauté the shallots or onion and garlic for about 5 minutes, until softened and golden brown.

4 In a large bowl, mix together the rice, shallots or onion, garlic, coriander, crabmeat, fish sauce or soy sauce, coconut milk, eggs and curry paste. Season.

5 Divide the mixture between the ramekins. Bake for 25–30 minutes, until set.

6 Leave to cool slightly, then turn them out and serve, garnished with finely sliced spring onions, red chilli and fresh coriander.

Eat wisely It can be tempting to buy ready made, shop bought varieties of fish cakes or fish fingers as a quick and easy family meal. However, making your own version, like in the recipe above, tastes better – and the extra effort is minimal.

Greek Spinach and Filo Pie

This Greek dish, also called Spanakopita, is popular all over the Mediterranean.

Serves 4

500 g (1 lb 2 oz) spinach, washed, tough
  stems removed and chopped
calorie controlled cooking spray
1 onion, chopped finely
a bunch of spring onions, chopped finely,
  including the green tops
a small bunch of flat leaf parsley,
  chopped finely
a small bunch of dill, chopped finely
¼ teaspoon grated nutmeg
100 g (3½ oz) low fat soft cheese
100 g (3½ oz) plain cottage cheese
8 x 15 g filo pastry sheets
salt and freshly ground black pepper

3 *ProPoints* values per serving
14 *ProPoints* values per recipe

C   **235 calories** per serving

Takes **30 minutes** to prepare,
45 minutes to cook

V

*   not recommended

1   Preheat the oven to Gas Mark 3/160°C/fan oven 140°C. Place the spinach in a lidded saucepan, cover and cook for 4 minutes until completely wilted. Transfer to a colander, press down with a wooden spoon to extract the moisture, then place it in a large bowl.

2   Spray a non stick frying pan with the cooking spray and sauté the onion for 5 minutes, stirring occasionally. Add the spring onions and cook for a further 2 minutes. Add them to the spinach with the herbs, nutmeg, seasoning and cheeses. Beat everything together with a wooden spoon.

3   Spray a metal 23 cm (9 inch) square baking tin or ovenproof dish with some more of the cooking spray. Cover the bottom of the tray with five sheets of filo pastry, one on top of the other, spraying each with a little cooking spray as you lay them down, and folding them up and over the sides of the dish.

4   Spread the spinach mixture over the filo, then cover with the remaining three sheets, spraying between each layer as well as on top.

5   Score through the top sheets of pastry with a knife to make triangle shaped portions, which will make cutting them up easier later (cut diagonally to the right and then to the left). Sprinkle with a little water to prevent the pastry curling and brush lightly to spread the water evenly.

6   Bake for 45 minutes until golden and crispy. Allow to stand for a few minutes before cutting into portions and serving.

Tip To prevent the filo pastry drying out while you are working, cover any unused sheets with a damp tea towel.

Soufflé Baked Potatoes

Simple baked potatoes take on an exciting new character with a light cheese and onion filling. Serve these with a crisp zero *ProPoints* value salad.

Serves 4

4 large (approx 300 g/10½ oz each) baking potatoes
calorie controlled cooking spray
a large bunch of spring onions, sliced finely
8 tablespoons skimmed milk
100 g (3½ oz) cherry tomatoes, quartered
2 egg whites
100 g (3½ oz) half fat Cheddar cheese, grated
salt and freshly ground black pepper

9 *ProPoints* values per serving
35 *ProPoints* values per recipe

332 calories per serving

Takes **15 minutes** to prepare,
1 hour 15 minutes to cook

V

* not recommended

1 Preheat the oven to Gas Mark 5/190°C/fan oven 170°C. Prick the potatoes all over with a fork and bake for 1 hour, or until soft.

2 Meanwhile spray a frying pan with the cooking spray and stir fry the spring onions until just tender and golden.

3 Cut the potatoes in half and scoop out the flesh into a large bowl. Add the milk and mash together until you have a smooth blend.

4 Stir in the spring onions and the tomatoes and season. In a clean, grease-free bowl, whisk the egg whites until stiff and fluffy and then fold carefully into the potato mixture with the grated cheese.

5 Place the potato skins on a baking tray and refill them with the potato mixture, piling up high. Bake for 10–15 minutes, until golden and hot. Serve immediately.

Tip If you don't have the time to bake your potato in the oven, then just pop it into the microwave on a high heat for 7–8 minutes until soft in the middle.

Macaroni Cheese Gratins

The whole family will love these cheesy little pots. And since they're made in individual dishes, everyone gets their own.

Serves 4

150 g (5½ oz) dried quick cook macaroni
2 tablespoons cornflour
300 ml (10 fl oz) skimmed milk
a pinch of ground nutmeg
75 g (2¾ oz) half fat Cheddar cheese, grated
calorie controlled cooking spray
1 tablespoon Worcestershire sauce
175 g (6 oz) carrots, peeled and grated
1 red onion, sliced thinly
1 courgette, grated
1 tablespoon dried breadcrumbs
15 g (½ oz) Parmesan cheese, grated
salt and freshly ground black pepper

To serve
Iceberg lettuce, shredded
cucumber, peeled and chopped

---

8 ProPoints values per serving
30 ProPoints values per recipe

282 calories per serving

Takes **20 minutes** to prepare,
35 minutes to cook

V

✱ recommended

1 Bring a pan of water to the boil, add the macaroni and cook according to the packet instructions. Drain well.

2 Meanwhile, in a saucepan, mix the cornflour with a little of the milk to form a thin paste. Heat the remaining milk until boiling and pour over the cornflour paste. Mix well and return to the heat. Cook, stirring for 2–3 minutes until you have a smooth thickened sauce.

3 Stir the nutmeg and grated cheese into the sauce. Then add the drained macaroni and stir well. Preheat the oven to Gas Mark 5/190°C/fan oven 170°C.

4 Spray a lidded non stick frying pan with the cooking spray and add the Worcestershire sauce, grated carrots, onion and courgette. Cover and cook for 2–3 minutes to just soften. Season to taste and then divide between four individual ramekins. Top with macaroni cheese.

5 Mix together the breadcrumbs and Parmesan cheese and sprinkle over the top. Bake for 15 minutes, then serve hot with a salad garnish.

Cooking basics How to cook pasta: place the pasta in a large saucepan. Add plenty of boiling water to allow the pasta to swell up and move (otherwise the pasta will become sticky). Cook until the pasta is just tender or al dente.

Tofu Kebabs with Peanut Sauce

Treat yourself to an exotic Thai style main meal, served with a luxurious peanut sauce.

Serves 4

2 x 200 g packets tofu, cut into bite size squares
4 tablespoons light soy sauce
2 teaspoons sesame oil
2 large garlic cloves, crushed
1 red pepper, de-seeded and cut into bite size squares
1 yellow pepper, de-seeded and cut into bite size squares
2 Little Gem lettuces, shredded, to serve

For the sauce

2 spring onions, chopped finely
½ teaspoon chilli powder
1 teaspoon caster sugar
4 teaspoons white wine vinegar
2 tablespoons crunchy peanut butter

6 _ProPoints_ values per serving
26 _ProPoints_ values per recipe

319 calories per serving

Takes **30 minutes** to prepare

V

✳ not recommended

1 Mix the tofu together with 2 tablespoons of the soy sauce, the sesame oil and garlic. Leave it to marinate for 5 minutes.

2 Thread the tofu and pepper pieces alternately on to wooden satay sticks.

3 In a small saucepan, place the sauce ingredients together with the remaining soy sauce and heat for 2–3 minutes until just hot and blended together.

4 Preheat the grill to a high heat. Grill the tofu kebabs for about 5–6 minutes, turning them once, until they are crispy. Serve the kebabs on the shredded lettuce with the sauce spooned over.

Cooking basics How to make the most of tofu: tofu doesn't have much flavour, but it absorbs the flavours it is cooked with like a sponge. Always allow enough time to marinate it properly and use liquid marinades, such as soy sauce, that will soak into the tofu.

Welsh Rarebit

It's hard to find a more classic combination than simple toast with cheese. This recipe is recognised all over the world as one of the great simple dishes. It's quick, easy to make and inexpensive, so it's a favourite with families.

Serves 4

100 g (3½ oz) low fat soft cheese with garlic and herbs
40 g (1½ oz) Caerphilly, grated finely
a few drops of mushroom ketchup or soy sauce
½ teaspoon wholegrain mustard
4 medium slices white or wholemeal bread
4 tomatoes, sliced
freshly ground black pepper
salad leaves, to garnish (optional)

€. **4 ProPoints** values per serving
16 ProPoints values per recipe

C **141 calories** per serving

⏱ Takes **20 minutes**

V

* not recommended

1 Preheat the grill to a medium heat.

2 In a small bowl, mix together the soft cheese, Caerphilly, mushroom ketchup or soy sauce and mustard. Season with a little black pepper.

3 Lightly toast the bread on both sides. Spread the cheese mixture on one side and then grill until golden and bubbling.

4 Serve at once with the tomatoes, garnished with salad leaves, if using.

Variations Use plain low fat soft cheese if you prefer and, if you want to spice up your Welsh rarebit, add a few drops of chilli sauce instead of the mushroom ketchup or soy sauce, for the same **ProPoints** values.

For a more substantial meal, top with well-drained lightly cooked spinach and a poached egg. The **ProPoints** values per serving will be 6.

Eat wisely For many of us cheese is our downfall – if it's in the fridge we'll eat it. A great solution is to grate your cheese into weighed out portions (e.g. 40 g/1½ oz) and then store these individual portions in bags in the freezer. When you want to use it, simply take out a bag and let it thaw for about an hour before using.

Turkey and Spinach Samosas

These are great to take on a picnic or in your lunchbox to the office. If you love really spicy food then just increase the chilli powder to your liking. Try serving these samosas with a crisp green salad for no additional *ProPoints* values.

Makes 15

calorie controlled cooking spray
1 small onion, diced finely
1 garlic clove, crushed
280 g (9¾ oz) turkey mince
1 teaspoon ground cumin
1 teaspoon ground coriander
1 teaspoon chilli powder
½ teaspoon ground ginger
175 g (6 oz) frozen chopped spinach, defrosted and drained
15 x 25 x 43 cm (10 x 17 inches) filo pastry sheets
salt and freshly ground black pepper

2 *ProPoints* values per serving
25 *ProPoints* values per recipe

C 75 calories per serving

Takes **35 minutes** to prepare, **15 minutes** to cook

* recommended for up to 1 month

1 Preheat the oven to Gas Mark 6/ 200°C/fan oven 180°C. Spray a medium saucepan with the cooking spray. Add the onion, garlic and turkey mince and cook for 5–6 minutes, stirring occasionally to brown the meat.

2 Add the spices and stir well before adding the spinach and seasoning. Mix together and heat to a gentle simmer. Simmer for 15 minutes.

3 Leave the mixture to cool slightly. Lay the filo pastry on the work surface. Lay one sheet on a chopping board large enough for the whole sheet. Spray the pastry with the cooking spray and then lay another sheet on top. Repeat this until you have three sheets of filo on top of each other.

4 Cut the stack of filo sheets lengthways into three.

5 Place a heaped tablespoon of the turkey and spinach mixture at the bottom of each strip of pastry. To fold into a samosa shape, lift one of the corners at the bottom of the pastry strip (nearest the filling) and bring it diagonally over the filling to the other side. This will give you a triangle shape. Pick up the point of the triangle and fold the filled pastry over diagonally. Keep folding over and over until you reach the top of the pastry strip and have a triangular samosa.

6 Repeat the process with the remaining pastry and turkey mixture to make 15 samosas.

7 Place the samosas on a baking tray and spray them with the cooking spray.

8 Bake the samosas in the oven for 15 minutes until golden.

Spring Rolls

These tasty, crunchy vegetable and prawn rolls have all the flavour of those served in Chinese restaurants, but they are only a fraction of the *ProPoints* values since they are baked and not deep fried.

Serves 4

calorie controlled cooking spray

100 g (3½ oz) carrots, peeled and sliced into thin strips

100 g (3½ oz) white cabbage, shredded

1 small red pepper, de-seeded and sliced thinly

100 g (3½ oz) fresh prawns, peeled

100 g (3½ oz) fresh beansprouts

2 tablespoons dark soy sauce, plus extra for dipping

¼ teaspoon Chinese five spice

8 x 15 g filo pastry sheets

---

3 *ProPoints* values per serving
10 *ProPoints* values per recipe

136 calories per serving

Takes **20 minutes** to prepare,
15 minutes to cook

* not recommended

1 Spray a large frying pan with the cooking spray, add the carrots, cabbage, red pepper, prawns, beansprouts, soy sauce and Chinese five spice and stir fry for 2 minutes. Remove the pan from the heat and allow the mixture to cool a little.

2 Preheat the oven to Gas Mark 5/190°C/fan oven 170°C. Line a baking tray with non stick baking parchment.

3 Spray a sheet of filo pastry with a little cooking spray. Spoon some of the filling on to one end of the pastry sheet. Roll the pastry up, tucking in the edges to enclose the filling so that you end up with a sausage shape. Repeat this process with the remaining pastry sheets until you have eight spring rolls.

4 Place the spring rolls on the baking tray and bake for 10 minutes until they are golden and crispy. Serve them hot with extra soy sauce for dipping, allowing two spring rolls per person.

Store cupboard ideas Soy sauce is an essential condiment, particularly if you like Oriental food. You can use it to colour and flavour marinades, dips and sauces. Light soy sauce has a delicate, salty flavour that goes well with white meats and seafood. Use dark soy sauce, which is thicker, richer but less salty, with meats or in stews.

Veggie Burgers

Delicious burgers, stuffed full of vegetables and served with a tasty Californian salsa.

Serves 4

400 g (14 oz) potatoes, peeled and quartered
500 g (1 lb 2 oz) mixed zero *ProPoints* value
  vegetables
calorie controlled cooking spray
2 leeks, chopped roughly
1 garlic clove, chopped
2 tablespoons soy sauce
1 tablespoon tomato purée
1 egg, beaten
a small bunch of fresh parsley, chopped
salt and freshly ground black pepper

For the salsa

100 g (3½ oz) cherry tomatoes, quartered
½ cucumber, diced finely
2 tablespoons tomato juice
1 small red onion, chopped finely
1 teaspoon horseradish sauce

3 *ProPoints* values per serving
12 *ProPoints* values per recipe

208 calories per serving

Takes **30 minutes**

V

✳ not recommended

1 Bring a pan of water to the boil, add the potatoes and cook for 15 minutes until tender, then drain. Meanwhile, cook the mixed vegetables in boiling water for 5 minutes and drain.

2 Heat a non stick frying pan and spray with the cooking spray. Fry the leeks and garlic for 10 minutes until softened and golden.

3 Mash the potatoes, then add the vegetables and other ingredients, including the cooked leeks and garlic. Season and mix well.

4 Shape the mixture into eight burgers. Heat a large non stick frying pan and spray with the cooking spray. Fry the burgers for 4–5 minutes on each side.

5 Meanwhile, mix all the salsa ingredients together in a bowl. Serve two burgers each with the salsa.

Simply Quiche

This scrumptious version of quiche Lorraine has far fewer *ProPoints* values than the original. Serve hot or cold with a zero *ProPoints* value mixed salad or vegetables.

Serves 4

4 medium slices bread
4 teaspoons low fat spread
2 rashers lean back bacon
2 eggs, beaten
220 g (7½ oz) low fat cottage cheese
2 tablespoons finely chopped onion
salt and freshly ground black pepper

5 *ProPoints* values per serving
22 *ProPoints* values per recipe

203 calories per serving

Takes **10 minutes** to prepare,
15–20 minutes to cook

✳ recommended

1 Preheat the oven to Gas Mark 6/200°C/fan oven 180°C. Flatten the slices of bread with a rolling pin until thin, then spread with the low fat spread. Use the slices (spread side up) to line a flan case, about 23 cm (9 inches) in diameter.

2 Grill the bacon rashers until crisp, then snip into small pieces. Mix with the eggs, cottage cheese and onion. Season.

3 Pour the mixture into the bread-lined flan case. Bake in the centre of the oven until set, about 20 minutes.

Tip For individual portions, cook the quiche in Yorkshire pudding tins or tartlet tins.

Variation For a vegetarian version, omit the bacon and use some chopped zero *ProPoints* value vegetables instead – courgettes and peppers would be ideal – for the same *ProPoints* values per serving.

Minced Meat Kebabs

On the streets of Morocco, Tunisia and Algeria, these fragrant kebabs are served in warmed pitta breads with a sprinkling of salt and cumin.

Serves 4

400 g (14 oz) lean minced lamb
a small bunch of fresh parsley, chopped
a small bunch of fresh coriander, chopped
1 onion, chopped finely
½ teaspoon ground allspice
¼ teaspoon cayenne pepper
1 teaspoon ground cumin
1 teaspoon paprika
calorie controlled cooking spray
salt and freshly ground black pepper
4 medium pitta breads, to serve

10 *ProPoints* values per serving
40 *ProPoints* values per recipe

210 **calories** per serving

Takes **30 minutes** + **1 hour** chilling

not recommended

1 Mix all the ingredients, except the cooking spray and pitta breads, to a smooth paste in a bowl.

2 With moistened hands, take generous tablespoons of the paste and mould it into 10 cm (4 inch) long finger shapes around four wooden or metal skewers. Refrigerate for 1 hour.

3 Preheat the grill and cover the grill pan with foil. Spray the skewers with the cooking spray, then grill for 4 minutes on each side. To serve, slice each pitta bread open and slide the kebabs off the skewers into the pittas.

Tips If the mince falls off the skewers in step 2, put it in the fridge for 30 minutes and try again.

If using wooden skewers, soak them in hot water for 10 minutes before using so that they will not burn under the grill.

Fish Goujons with Tartare Sauce

Serve these crisp coated fish pieces as finger food, with the creamy tartare sauce as a dip.

Serves 6

100 g (3½ oz) plaice, skinned and cut into thick strips

50 g (1¾ oz) plain flour, seasoned with ½ teaspoon chilli powder

2 large egg whites, beaten

300 g (10½ oz) fresh breadcrumbs

lemon wedges, to serve

For the tartare sauce

100 g (3½ oz) low fat soft cheese

200 ml (7 fl oz) very low fat plain fromage frais

2 tablespoons capers, rinsed and squeezed to remove excess vinegar

4 small gherkins, chopped finely

2 spring onions, chopped finely

a small bunch of fresh dill or fennel, chopped

salt and freshly ground black pepper

5 ProPoints values per serving
30 ProPoints values per recipe

201 calories per serving

Takes **35 minutes**

not recommended

1 Preheat the grill to a medium heat. Dip some of the fish strips first in the chilli flour, then in the egg whites and finally in the breadcrumbs. Spread out on a grill pan lined with foil.

2 Grill the goujons until golden and crisp and cooked through, turning over once or twice to brown all over. Repeat with the remaining fish strips.

3 Meanwhile, make the tartare sauce by beating together the soft cheese and fromage frais and then stirring in all the other ingredients with some seasoning. Tip into a serving bowl and serve with the goujons and the lemon wedges to squeeze over.

BBQ Chicken Drumsticks

A perfect family lunch for a summer weekend.

Makes 12 drumsticks

12 x 47 g (1¾ oz) skinless chicken drumsticks

For the marinade

2 garlic cloves, crushed

2.5 cm (1 inch) fresh root ginger, grated

finely grated zest of 2 oranges

juice of an orange

1 small red chilli, de-seeded and chopped finely

2 tablespoons clear honey

2 tablespoons soy sauce

2 tablespoons tomato purée

½ tablespoon sesame oil

**2 *ProPoints* values per serving
21 *ProPoints* values per recipe**

88 calories per serving

Takes **10 minutes** to prepare + **4 hours** marinating, **15–25 minutes** to cook

recommended

1 Mix all the marinade ingredients together in a small bowl. Put the drumsticks in a non-metallic dish, add the marinade and turn the drumsticks to make sure they are well coated. Leave to marinate in the refrigerator for at least 4 hours, but preferably overnight.

2 Preheat the grill to a medium heat or ensure your barbecue is ready. Cook the drumsticks for 15–25 minutes, or until they are thoroughly cooked and golden brown. (A grill will take longer than a hot barbecue.)

Cooking basics To cut and de-seed chillies: carefully slice the chilli in half vertically. Use a teaspoon to scrape out the seeds and throw them away. Cut away the white membrane. Slice the chillies very finely and add to the dish. Wash your hands thoroughly.

Tandoori Turkey Bites

Kids love these spicy little turkey bites.

Serves 4

2 tablespoons tandoori paste
2 teaspoons lemon juice
6 tablespoons low fat natural yogurt
2 tablespoons chopped fresh mint
450 g (1 lb) turkey steaks, cut into
  2.5 cm (1 inch) chunks

5 *ProPoints* values per serving
21 *ProPoints* values per recipe

151 calories per serving

Takes **10 minutes** to prepare + **1–4 hours**
marinating, **15 minutes** to cook

recommended

1 Mix together the tandoori paste, lemon juice, yogurt and mint in a non-metallic bowl.

2 Add the turkey, stir well, then cover and refrigerate for 1–4 hours. The longer the meat is left to marinate, the more intense the flavour will be.

3 Preheat the grill to high or ensure your barbecue is ready. Thread the cubes of turkey on to eight skewers and cook for about 15 minutes, turning occasionally. Serve immediately.

Tip Wooden kebab sticks should be soaked in hot water for about 10 minutes before use, to prevent them from burning when grilling.

Variation Balti curry paste can be used instead of tandoori paste, for the same *ProPoints* values.

Roast Chicken with Rosemary and Lemon Potatoes

A Sunday lunch regular – this roast never fails to please.

Serves 4

400 g (14 oz) potatoes, cut into wedges
1.5 kg (3 lb 5 oz) whole chicken
2 lemons, 1 cut into wedges the other cut in half
a small bunch of rosemary, leaves removed from the stalks and chopped
calorie controlled cooking spray
300 ml (10 fl oz) chicken stock
salt and freshly ground black pepper

6 *ProPoints* values per serving
26 *ProPoints* values per recipe

345 calories per serving

Takes **35 minutes** to prepare,
1 hour 15 minutes to cook

✳ not recommended

1 Bring a pan of water to the boil add the potatoes and parboil for 15–20 minutes. Drain.

2 Preheat the oven to Gas Mark 6/200°C/fan oven 180°C. Place the chicken in a large roasting tray and season all over. Squeeze the juice from the halved lemon over the skin of the chicken and then place the squeezed lemon 'shells' inside the cavity of the chicken with half the rosemary.

3 Place the lemon wedges and parboiled potatoes around the bird. Spray with the cooking spray, season and sprinkle with the remaining rosemary. Roast for 1¼ hours, basting occasionally with any juices in the tray, turning and basting the potatoes at the same time.

4 To test if the chicken is cooked, stick a skewer or knife into the meatiest portion of one of the thighs. The juices should run clear.

5 When cooked, remove the chicken from the roasting tray to a carving board, cover with foil and keep warm while you make the gravy.

6 To make the gravy, remove the potatoes and lemon wedges to serving bowls and keep warm. Drain off any excess fat and place the roasting tray on the hob. Heat until the juices boil and then add the stock.

7 Scrape up any juices stuck to the tin with a wooden spoon or spatula and boil rapidly for a few minutes until reduced a little. Strain the gravy into a jug and serve with three skinless slices of chicken per person, garnished with the roasted lemon wedges and the roast potatoes.

Beef Fillet with Horseradish Crust

What's more traditional than roast beef and Yorkshire pudding? A real family treat.

Serves 8

1 kg (2 lb 4 oz) lean fillet of beef, in one
 piece or boned and rolled sirloin
150 g (5½ oz) mushrooms, chopped
a bunch of rosemary, chopped finely
4 tablespoons horseradish sauce
200 g (7 oz) fresh breadcrumbs
calorie controlled cooking spray
salt and freshly ground black pepper

For the Yorkshire puddings

100 g (3½ oz) plain flour
1 egg
300 ml (10 fl oz) skimmed milk

For the gravy

2 teaspoons plain flour
300 ml (10 fl oz) vegetable stock

---

8 *ProPoints* values per serving
68 *ProPoints* values per recipe

370 calories per serving

Takes **20 minutes** to prepare, **1 hour** to
cook + **10 minutes** resting time

* not recommended

1 Preheat the oven to Gas Mark 7/220°C/fan oven 200°C. With a sharp knife make a slit along the side of the fillet then open it up to make a pocket. Mix the mushrooms with half the rosemary and seasoning and stuff inside the fillet.

2 Season the outside of the fillet and then spread all over with the horseradish sauce. Spread the breadcrumbs on a large plate and roll the fillet in them until they are stuck all over.

3 Spray a roasting tin with the cooking spray and place the fillet in it. Cover with a piece of foil.

4 Roast the beef on a lower shelf for 30 minutes. Take off the foil and brown for a further 15 minutes for a medium cooked fillet. For a well done fillet, brown for 30 minutes. Remove the beef from the oven and place on a carving board, loosely covered with the foil again, to keep warm and allow to rest for 10 minutes before carving.

5 Meanwhile, for the Yorkshire puddings, prepare the batter by mixing the flour with a pinch of salt in a large bowl. Make a well in the middle and crack in the egg, add the milk and 100 ml (3½ fl oz) of water. Gradually stir in the flour until you have a smooth batter.

6 Put a baking tin or patty tin with 12 individual moulds in the oven, on the top shelf, for 5 minutes, until very hot. Using an oven glove remove the tin from the oven, spray with the cooking spray and quickly pour in the batter. Return it to the top shelf and bake for 40 minutes, until the puddings are risen and golden. Do not open the oven door while they are cooking.

7 To make the gravy, pour off any fat in the roasting tin and then set it on the hob. Sprinkle over the flour and mix it in with the juices using a wooden spatula. Add the remaining rosemary and stock and boil rapidly, scraping up any stuck on juices with the spatula. Season and pour into a serving jug.

Simply
Suppers

There's nothing better at the end of the day than quick and easy suppers that are satisfying and full of flavour. Try pasta dishes, such as Spinach and Ricotta Cannelloni; one-pot meals, such as Sausage and Bean Hotpot; recipes from around the world, like Mediterranean Turkey Rolls; and modern twists on family favourites, such as Mini Toad in the Hole.

Make the most of your evenings by having supper together as a family

Prawn and Chilli Tagliatelle

A hot and spicy recipe with big juicy prawns. Temper the heat with a cooling yogurt sauce.

Serves 4

225 g (8 oz) dried tagliatelle
calorie controlled cooking spray
1 onion, chopped
1 garlic clove, crushed
400 g can chopped tomatoes
1 tablespoon hot chilli sauce
20 tiger prawns, shelled, defrosted if frozen,
  with tail tip left on (see Tip)
1 tablespoon coriander, freshly chopped
salt and freshly ground black pepper

For the dip

150 g pot 0% fat Greek yogurt
1 tablespoon chopped fresh mint
finely grated zest of ½ a lemon

7 *ProPoints* values per serving
28 *ProPoints* values per recipe

275 calories per serving

Takes **20 minutes**

not recommended

1 Bring a large pan of water to the boil, add the tagliatelle and cook for 10–12 minutes or according to the packet instructions.

2 Meanwhile, for the dip, mix the yogurt, mint and lemon zest together and set aside.

3 Spray a non stick saucepan with the cooking spray and heat over a medium heat until sizzling. Add the onion and cook for 5 minutes until softened, then add the garlic and cook for a further 2 minutes.

4 Stir in the tomatoes and chilli sauce, reduce the heat and simmer for 5 minutes until thickened. Stir in the prawns and cook for 2 minutes until hot.

5 Drain the tagliatelle, pour over the prawn sauce and toss to mix. Season and stir in the coriander. Serve with the yoghurt sauce as a dip for the prawns.

Tips If you prefer a creamy sauce, simply combine the yogurt mixture with the tomato sauce.

If you leave the tails on the prawns, they are easier to pick up and dip into the yogurt.

Variation Adjust the amount of chilli sauce to your liking.

Mushroom and Leek Macaroni

Cream and wine go wonderfully well together and this recipe makes the most of half fat crème fraîche to give a really creamy, tasty sauce.

Serves 4

225 g (8 oz) dried quick cook macaroni
calorie controlled cooking spray
2 leeks, trimmed, washed and sliced
250 g (9 oz) mixed mushrooms (e.g. button, chestnut, oyster), sliced
2 garlic cloves, crushed
125 ml (4 fl oz) dry white wine
1 tablespoon mushroom ketchup or soy sauce
4 tablespoons half fat crème fraîche
3 tablespoons chopped fresh parsley, plus extra to garnish
salt and freshly ground black pepper

8 ProPoints values per serving
31 ProPoints values per recipe

300 calories per serving

Takes **20 minutes**

V

✳ not recommended

1 Bring a large pan of water to the boil, add the macaroni and cook for 6–7 minutes or according to the packet instructions. Drain and rinse with boiling water.

2 Meanwhile, spray a frying pan with the cooking spray, add the leeks and mushrooms and stir fry over a medium heat for 5 minutes until softened. Add the garlic and continue cooking for 2 minutes until the mushroom juices have evaporated.

3 Add the wine and mushroom ketchup or soy sauce and simmer over a medium heat to reduce the liquid by half. Turn down the heat and stir in the crème fraîche and parsley. Add the macaroni and heat for 2 minutes until piping hot. Season and serve garnished with extra parsley.

Tip Make this a store cupboard supper by using dried mushrooms instead of fresh.

Variation Tarragon has a lovely subtle aniseed-like flavour; try substituting it for the parsley.

Penne with Meatballs

A classic recipe with a twist. In this version, turkey mince replaces beef mince, which reduces the *ProPoints* values without reducing the delicious flavours.

Serves 4

For the meatballs
calorie controlled cooking spray
1 onion, chopped finely
1 garlic clove, crushed
300 g (10½ oz) turkey mince
1 teaspoon dried mixed herbs
200 g (7 oz) dried penne
salt and freshly ground black pepper

For the sauce
1 garlic clove, crushed
2 tablespoons shredded basil leaves, plus
  extra for garnish
250 g (9 oz) passata

7 *ProPoints* values per serving
30 *ProPoints* values per recipe

300 calories per serving

Takes **40 minutes** to prepare and cook
+ **10 minutes** chilling

recommended (meatballs only)

1 Spray a large non stick frying pan with the cooking spray and heat over a medium heat until hot. Add the onion and cook, stirring, for 5 minutes until beginning to brown. Add the garlic and cook for a further 2 minutes. Remove from the heat and let it cool slightly.

2 Place the turkey mince in a large bowl with the onion and garlic mixture, herbs and seasoning, then mix it all together – you might find it easiest to mix with your hands.

3 Make 20 walnut sized balls, rolling them in your hands until smooth. Cover and chill for 10 minutes to help them bind together.

4 Bring a large pan of water to the boil, add the pasta and cook for 10–12 minutes or according to the packet instructions. Drain and rinse with boiling water.

5 Meanwhile, respray the frying pan with the cooking spray and cook the meatballs over a medium heat, turning frequently for 8 minutes until golden all over. For the sauce, add the garlic and the shredded basil to the pan with the meatballs and cook over a low heat for 2 minutes, then add the passata. Slowly bring to the boil, reduce the heat and simmer for 2–3 minutes until piping hot.

6 Divide the pasta between four bowls and serve the meatballs on top with the sauce drizzled over and garnished with the basil leaves.

Tips Wet your hands when rolling the meatballs as it makes the meatballs less sticky.

You can make the meatballs and cook them in advance, then simply heat them through in the sauce when you are ready to eat.

Spinach and Ricotta Cannelloni

The whole family will love this quick, filling and tasty dish.

Serves 4

4 sheets (188 g/7 oz) fresh lasagne, measuring 14½ x 20 cm (5¾ x 8 inches)

300 g (10½ oz) frozen spinach, defrosted and drained

220 g (7½ oz) ricotta

600 g (1 lb 5 oz) passata with herbs

salt and freshly ground black pepper

a handful of fresh basil leaves, torn, to garnish

7 *ProPoints* values per serving
27 *ProPoints* values per recipe

229 calories per serving

Takes **30 minutes**

V

* recommended

1 Preheat the oven to Gas Mark 6/200°C/fan oven 180°C. Halve each lasagne sheet to create eight rectangles approximately 7 x 10 cm (3 x 4 inches). Bring a large pan of water to the boil, add the lasagne and cook according to the packet instructions. Drain and keep warm.

2 Mix together the spinach and ricotta. Season to taste. Place a sheet of lasagne on a plate, put 2 tablespoons of the spinach mixture in a line in the centre and roll up. Repeat with the other sheets using all the mixture. Place the tubes in an ovenproof dish.

3 Pour the passata over the cannelloni. Bake for 15 minutes until bubbling. Serve garnished with the fresh basil leaves.

Eat wisely When you go to the effort of making a delicious family meal, such as this cannelloni, make it into more of an occasion. Turn off the TV and use the time to chat over the day. You'll find that you enjoy the food more too.

Creamy Chicken Bake

Pop this in the oven to cook while you enjoy time with the family.

Serves 4

calorie controlled cooking spray

300 g (10½ oz) skinless boneless chicken breast, diced

2 small courgettes, sliced

175 g (6 oz) dried fusilli

600 g (1 lb 5 oz) passata with herbs

200 g (7 oz) low fat soft cheese with garlic and herbs

8 *ProPoints* values per serving
30 *ProPoints* values per recipe

340 calories per serving

Takes **10 minutes** to prepare,
45 minutes to cook

* not recommended

1 Preheat the oven to Gas Mark 5/190ºC/fan oven 170ºC. Heat a frying pan until hot and then spray with the cooking spray. Add the chicken pieces and courgettes and stir fry for 3–5 minutes until the chicken is browned all over.

2 Meanwhile, bring a pan of water to the boil, add the pasta and cook for 2 minutes only. Drain.

3 Add the passata and 100 ml (3½ fl oz) of water to the chicken mixture and stir in. Bring to the boil.

4 Remove from the heat and add the pasta and soft cheese to the chicken. Pour into a baking dish, cover with foil and bake for 45 minutes until the chicken and pasta are cooked. Serve immediately on warmed plates.

Vegetable Risotto

An easy dish that you can put on and leave to cook while you get on with other things. It's guaranteed to fill everyone up and you can vary the vegetables according to your family's taste or what is seasonally available.

Serves 4

calorie controlled cooking spray
2 large onions, chopped finely
4 garlic cloves, crushed
2 courgettes, diced finely
2 red peppers, de-seeded and diced finely
450 g (1 lb) mushrooms, sliced
250 g (9 oz) dried long grain rice
500 ml (18 fl oz) passata
600 ml (20 fl oz) vegetable stock
salt and freshly ground black pepper

6 ProPoints values per serving
25 ProPoints values per recipe

325 calories per serving

Takes **20 minutes** to prepare,
30 minutes to cook

V

✳ recommended

1 Spray a large lidded saucepan with the cooking spray and then stir fry the onions and garlic until softened, adding a little water, if necessary, to prevent them from sticking.

2 Add the other vegetables and stir fry for a few minutes, until golden. Add all the remaining ingredients, stir together and bring to the boil.

3 Turn down to a low simmer and put the lid on. Leave to cook for 30 minutes or until the rice has absorbed all the water and is tender. Serve immediately on warmed plates.

Cooking basics Make your own vegetable stock: reserve all the trimmings and peel from vegetables and boil them in a pan with 1.2 litres (2 pints) of water, a handful of peppercorns, half an onion, a bay leaf and some herbs. Cook for 1 hour then remove from the heat and strain. The stock will keep in the fridge for a few days or can be frozen.

Sesame Chicken

This is great as a light and fast supper.

Serves 4

2 x 150 g (5½ oz) skinless boneless chicken breasts, cut in half lengthways
4 garlic cloves, sliced finely
2.5 cm (1 inch) fresh root ginger, grated finely
4 tablespoons soy sauce
zest and juice of 2 limes
2 teaspoons sesame oil

For the spinach salad

225 g (8 oz) baby spinach leaves
a small bunch of fresh mint, chopped roughly
a bunch of spring onions, sliced finely lengthways

1 Lay the chicken breasts between two pieces of baking parchment, cling film or foil and pound with a rolling pin until they become thin escalopes.

2 Place the garlic, ginger, soy sauce, lime zest and juice and sesame oil in a large bowl and add the chicken breasts. Toss the chicken in the marinade and then set aside for at least 5 minutes but preferably 30 minutes.

3 Meanwhile, divide the spinach, mint and spring onions between four serving plates or bowls.

4 Preheat the grill and line the grill tray with foil. Remove the chicken from the marinade and grill for 4–5 minutes on each side, or until cooked through and golden. Slice the chicken and place on top of the spinach salad.

5 Heat the leftover marinade in a small pan until boiling, then drizzle over the chicken and salad before serving.

3 *ProPoints* values per serving
11 *ProPoints* values per recipe

145 calories per serving

Takes **15 minutes** + marinating

* not recommended

Cooking basics How to prepare ginger: using a sharp knife, cut the length of ginger you need. Carefully slice off the skin. Holding the ginger at one end, slice it very thinly. Alternatively, use a cheese grater to grate the ginger into fine slices.

Sausage and Bean Hotpot

A one-pot recipe, this just needs some zero *ProPoints* value green vegetables to accompany it.

Serves 4

calorie controlled cooking spray
8 Weight Watchers premium pork sausages
2 onions, sliced
2 garlic cloves, crushed
1 teaspoon dried mixed herbs
400 g can chopped tomatoes
300 ml (10 fl oz) vegetable stock
2 x 410 g cans cannellini beans, drained and rinsed
salt and freshly ground black pepper

1 Heat the cooking spray in a lidded non stick frying pan and fry the sausages and onions for 5 minutes over a medium heat until browned.

2 Add the garlic and herbs and cook for 30 seconds, then stir in the remaining ingredients. Bring to a simmer, cover and cook for 10 minutes.

3 Remove the lid and cook for a final 5 minutes to thicken the sauce slightly.

7 *ProPoints* values per serving
28 *ProPoints* values per recipe

267 calories per serving

Takes **10 minutes** to prepare,
15 minutes to cook

✳ recommended

Vegetarian variation For a vegetarian version, simply substitute eight thick vegetarian sausages for the pork sausages, for the same *ProPoints* values per serving.

Family Fish Pie

An easy fish pie that's great for a midweek supper. Serve with your favourite zero *ProPoints* value vegetables, such as broccoli and carrots.

Serves 6

450 g (1 lb) floury potatoes, peeled and cut into chunks

450 g (1 lb) pumpkin or butternut squash, peeled, de-seeded and cut into chunks

600 ml (20 fl oz) skimmed milk

2 bay leaves

500 g (1 lb 2 oz) cod fillets

calorie controlled cooking spray

1 large onion, sliced

2 garlic cloves, crushed

4 celery sticks or a small fennel bulb, chopped finely

150 g (5½ oz) mushrooms, sliced

100 g (3½ oz) frozen sweetcorn or peas

2 tablespoons cornflour

a small bunch of fresh parsley, chopped

1 heaped teaspoon French mustard

100 g (3½ oz) half fat mature Cheddar cheese, grated

salt and freshly ground black pepper

---

7 *ProPoints* values per serving
39 *ProPoints* values per recipe

277 **calories** per serving

Takes **35 minutes** to prepare, **20 minutes** to cook

✴ not recommended

1. Bring a pan of water to the boil, add the potatoes and pumpkin or butternut squash and cook for 20 minutes, or until tender. Strain but reserve the cooking liquid. Mash the two together and season.

2. Meanwhile, in a large non stick frying pan, heat the milk with the bay leaves and fish fillets until it comes to the boil and then simmer for 1 minute, or until the fish is almost cooked through. Remove the fish to a plate and then strain the milk into a small saucepan and reserve.

3. Rinse the frying pan and spray with the cooking spray. Fry the onion and garlic for 5 minutes, until softened, adding 1–2 tablespoons of the reserved potato cooking liquid, if necessary, to prevent them from sticking.

4. Add the celery or fennel and a few more tablespoons of the potato cooking liquid and cook for a further 5 minutes. Add the mushrooms and cook on a high heat for 3 minutes, until the mushrooms start to give out their juices. Remove from the heat. This mixture needs to be dry, so drain off any juices.

5. Break up the fish, removing any skin and bones, and fold into the vegetables with the sweetcorn or peas. Transfer the whole mixture to a large baking dish.

6. Preheat the oven to Gas Mark 6/200°C/fan oven 180°C. Take a couple of tablespoons of the reserved milk and mix with the cornflour. Stir this paste back into the rest of the milk and bring to the boil, stirring, until it thickens; then add the parsley, mustard and seasoning.

7. Pour the parsley sauce over the fish mixture and fold gently together. Top with the potato and pumpkin mash. Scatter over the grated cheese and bake for 20 minutes, until the cheese is golden and bubbling.

Shepherd's Pie

Serve with plenty of zero *ProPoints* value vegetables: broccoli, cauliflower or cabbage would be ideal.

Serves 4

900 g (2 lb) potatoes, peeled and quartered
350 g (12 oz) lean lamb mince
1 large onion, chopped finely
1 large leek, chopped finely
1 carrot, peeled and chopped
225 g (8 oz) swede or turnip, peeled and chopped
450 ml (16 fl oz) lamb or vegetable stock
2 tablespoons cornflour
6 tablespoons skimmed milk
salt and freshly ground black pepper

11 *ProPoints* values per serving
45 *ProPoints* values per recipe

390 calories per serving

Takes 30 minutes to prepare, 50 minutes to cook

✳ recommended

1 Bring a pan of water to the boil, add the potatoes and cook for about 20 minutes, until tender.

2 Meanwhile, heat a large, lidded, non stick saucepan and add the lamb mince, a handful at a time, cooking over a high heat to seal and brown it.

3 Add the onion to the mince with the leek, carrot and swede or turnip and cook for about 3 minutes, stirring often. Pour in the stock, bring to the boil, cover and simmer for about 20 minutes.

4 Preheat the oven to Gas Mark 5/190°C/fan oven 170°C. Blend the cornflour with 3 or 4 tablespoons of cold water and stir into the lamb mixture. Cook until thickened for about 2 minutes. Remove from the heat.

5 Drain the potatoes and mash them. Add the milk and seasoning and beat vigorously with a wooden spoon until the potatoes are light and fluffy. Alternatively, use a hand held electric whisk to whisk the potatoes for a few moments.

6 Transfer the meat mixture to a 1.2 litre (2 pint) ovenproof dish and top with the mashed potato. Bake for 25–30 minutes until thoroughly heated and browned.

Vegetable Chilli

Bring the flavours of Mexico to your table with this easy-to-make tasty vegetarian chilli.

Serves 4

calorie controlled cooking spray
1 large onion, chopped
2 garlic cloves, crushed
3 celery sticks, chopped finely
1 large carrot, peeled and chopped finely
1 courgette, chopped
350 g packet Quorn mince
2–3 teaspoons medium chilli powder
400 g can chopped tomatoes
2 tablespoons tomato purée
215 g can red kidney beans, drained and
  rinsed
198 g can sweetcorn with peppers
300 ml (10 fl oz) hot vegetable stock
175 g (6 oz) dried long grain rice
salt and freshly ground black pepper

9 ProPoints values per serving
36 ProPoints values per recipe

375 calories per serving

Takes **15 minutes** to prepare,
30 minutes to cook

V

* recommended

1 Heat a large lidded saucepan and spray with the cooking spray. Add the onion, garlic, celery, carrot and courgette. Stir fry for 2–3 minutes.

2 Add the Quorn mince, chilli powder, tomatoes, tomato purée, kidney beans, sweetcorn with peppers and stock to the pan. Stir well and bring to the boil. Cover, reduce the heat and simmer for about 30 minutes, stirring from time to time.

3 Around 15 minutes before you are ready to serve bring a pan of water to the boil, add the rice and cook for about 12 minutes until tender, or according to the packet instructions. Drain well and rinse with boiling water.

4 Check the flavour of the chilli and season according to taste. Divide the cooked rice between four warmed serving plates and pile the cooked chilli on top. Serve at once.

Tips Cook spicy food according to your taste, adding extra chilli powder if you like things spicy, or use it sparingly if you prefer a milder flavour.

Cans of sweetcorn with peppers are available in supermarkets. Although not as quick, you could also use 150 g (5½ oz) of sweetcorn and 50 g (1¾ oz) of chopped peppers. The **ProPoints** values will remain the same.

Szechuan Beef Stir Fry

A tasty stir fry with the most tender beef.

Serves 4

250 g (9 oz) lean beef braising steak, cut into thin strips
1 teaspoon bicarbonate of soda

For the sauce

1 teaspoon cornflour
2 tablespoons tomato purée
1 tablespoon rice or wine vinegar
1 teaspoon chilli powder
1 teaspoon caster sugar
2 teaspoons soy sauce

For the stir fry

2 teaspoons peanut oil
2 garlic cloves, sliced into slivers
2.5 cm (1 inch) fresh root ginger, sliced into fine matchsticks
a bunch of spring onions, sliced finely
200 g (7 oz) mushrooms, preferably oyster, sliced finely
125 g can water chestnuts, drained

---

3 *ProPoints* values per serving
13 *ProPoints* values per recipe

160 calories per serving

Takes **35 minutes** to prepare
+ 4 hours marinating

* recommended

1 Put the beef in a bowl with the bicarbonate of soda and just enough water to cover. Leave to marinate in the refrigerator for about 4 hours.

2 In a bowl, mix the cornflour into a paste with 2 tablespoons of water and then mix in all the other sauce ingredients.

3 When ready to cook, drain the beef and pat dry on kitchen towel. Heat the oil in a large frying pan or wok until just smoking then add the beef and toss around the pan for 2 minutes. Add the garlic and ginger and stir fry for another minute.

4 Add all the other ingredients, toss and stir fry over a high heat for 2 minutes. Give the sauce ingredients a stir and pour over. Bring to the boil, stir and serve.

Store cupboard ideas Stir fries are fantastic, flavoursome and a very quick dish to make. Most supermarkets sell ready prepared fresh zero *ProPoints* value stir fry vegetables quite cheaply, so rather than chopping and preparing your own you can just throw the whole packet into the pan for a quick and tasty meal.

Maple and Mustard Chicken Tray-bake

Great for a mid-week roast, this also cuts down on washing up as it's all cooked together in one tray.

Serves 4

800 g (1 lb 11 oz) small new potatoes, halved
2 red onions, chopped roughly
2 courgettes, chopped roughly
1 tablespoon olive oil
4 x 125 g (4½ oz) skinless boneless chicken breasts
2 tablespoons maple syrup
1 heaped tablespoon wholegrain mustard
juice of a lemon
250 g (9 oz) cherry tomatoes
salt and freshly ground black pepper

9 ProPoints values per serving
37 ProPoints values per recipe

387 calories per serving

Takes **15 minutes** to prepare,
50 minutes to cook

✳ not recommended

1 Preheat the oven to Gas Mark 6/200°C/fan oven 180°C. Parboil the potatoes in boiling water for 10 minutes. Drain and mix with the onions, courgettes, olive oil and seasoning in a large roasting tin. Place in the oven to cook for 15 minutes.

2 Stir the vegetables around, season the chicken breasts and add to the roasting tin. Roast for a further 10 minutes.

3 Mix the maple syrup with the mustard and lemon juice. Stir the vegetables around again, adding the tomatoes, and drizzle the maple mustard glaze all over the chicken and vegetables.

4 Roast for a final 15 minutes.

Store cupboard ideas Onions are an essential store cupboard ingredient and you should always try to keep a stock of them in your kitchen. They are a wonderful base to almost any dish – adding flavour and texture. Experiment to find your favourite – white onions, red onions, shallots, spring onions. Try roasting, sweating, frying – add to casseroles and stir fries or use them in a delicious roast dish like in the recipe above.

Garlic Roast Pork with Mash

Creamy, garlicky mash topped with garlic pork chops.

Serves 4

450 g (1 lb) pork loin, visible fat removed
2 garlic bulbs, unpeeled
4 garlic cloves, chopped
600 g (1 lb 5 oz) potatoes, peeled and chopped
125 ml (4 fl oz) skimmed milk
salt and freshly ground black pepper
200 g (7 oz) broccoli, cut into florets and
  steamed or boiled, to serve

11 *ProPoints* values per serving
44 *ProPoints* values per recipe

366 **calories** per serving

Takes **20 minutes** to prepare,
50 minutes to cook

* not recommended

1 Preheat the oven to Gas Mark 7/220°C/fan oven 200°C.

2 Make slits between the pork flesh and the bones and place the meat in a baking dish with the garlic bulbs. Stuff the chopped garlic into the slits in the meat and rub the joint with seasoning. Roast for 25 minutes until golden.

3 Remove the garlic bulbs, set aside and reduce the oven temperature to Gas Mark 4/180°C/fan oven 160°C. Cook the pork for another 25–35 minutes.

4 Meanwhile, cook the potatoes in a pan of boiling water until tender. Drain and add the skimmed milk. Squeeze out the cooked garlic from the bulbs, add to the pototoes and mash together until creamy.

5 Serve the pork, sliced into thick pieces on a bed of garlicky mash with the steamed or boiled broccoli.

Store cupboard ideas Garlic is indispensable in cooking – so always keep some bulbs in the fridge. Choose fresh, plump looking garlic with a white skin and a fat neck, as these will have a more delicate flavour. Stick to the specified amount in recipes until you know your taste well – too much garlic will quickly overpower the other flavours in the dish.

Braised Lamb Chops

This makes a traditional and satisfying midweek dinner with a minimum of hassle.

Serves 4

2 tablespoons plain flour

4 x 130 g (4½ oz) lamb leg chops, trimmed
  of visible fat

calorie controlled cooking spray

1 large onion, sliced

a small bunch of fresh thyme or marjoram

150 ml (5 fl oz) stock

450 g (1 lb) sweet potatoes, peeled and
  sliced thickly

100 g (3½ oz) mushrooms, sliced

4 beef tomatoes, sliced thickly

salt and freshly ground black pepper

10 *ProPoints* values per serving
38 *ProPoints* values per recipe

355 calories per serving

Takes **30 minutes** to prepare,
1 hour to cook

✳ recommended

1 Put the flour on a plate, season, then roll the chops in it. Heat a large lidded frying pan and spray with the cooking spray. Brown the lamb for a few minutes on each side then remove from the pan to a plate and set aside.

2 Spray the pan with the cooking spray again and fry the onion for 4 minutes until softened. Add the herbs and the stock, scraping up any juices stuck to the bottom of the pan.

3 Arrange a layer of the sweet potato slices on the bottom of the pan and then top with the lamb. Cover and cook gently for 45 minutes.

4 Add the mushrooms and then a layer of tomato slices. Season and cook for another 15 minutes then serve.

Variation Use ordinary potatoes rather than sweet ones for a more traditional dish. The *ProPoints* values per serving will be 9.

Store cupboard ideas Stock is an essential ingredient when eating the Weight Watchers way. You should always keep a good supply – either buy stock cubes from the supermarket or make your own. You'll find that stock is often used as a base for soups, casseroles or curries.

One Pot Goulash

This is a great midweek dish as you can assemble it in advance up to the point where you put the casserole in the oven, and then just cook it when you need it. Dill isn't a traditional Hungarian accompaniment, but it is delicious with the tender slow cooked beef.

Serves 4

2 teaspoons caraway seeds
600 g (1 lb 5 oz) new potatoes
calorie controlled cooking spray
500 g (1 lb 2 oz) lean braising steak, cubed
2 large onions, chopped
2 garlic cloves, crushed
2 red peppers, de-seeded and cut into
  chunks
1 teaspoon hot smoked paprika (see Tip)
2 x 400 g cans chopped tomatoes
200 ml (7 fl oz) beef stock
2 tablespoons chopped fresh dill (optional)
salt and freshly ground black pepper
4 tablespoons low fat natural yogurt,
  to serve

9 *ProPoints* values per serving
35 *ProPoints* values per recipe

395 calories per serving

Takes **15 minutes** to prepare,
1¾ hours to cook

＊ recommended

1 Preheat the oven to Gas Mark 4/180°C/fan oven 160°C. Using a pestle and mortar or a heavy rolling pin, crush the caraway seeds to release their aroma. Wash the potatoes and cut any large ones in two – leave the rest whole. Put the seeds and potatoes to one side.

2 Spray a large, lidded, flame and ovenproof casserole dish with the cooking spray and fry the beef for a few minutes until sealed and browned on all sides. You may need to do this in batches. Remove the beef from the pan and set aside.

3 If necessary, spray the pan again and then add the onions, garlic and peppers. Fry for 2–3 minutes to soften them. Return the beef to the pan and stir in the paprika, crushed caraway seeds, tomatoes, stock and potatoes.

4 Put the lid on the casserole dish, place it in the oven and cook for 1¾ hours or until the meat is tender. Stir occasionally.

5 Before serving, check the seasoning and stir in the chopped dill, if using. Divide between four large, warmed bowls and top each with a tablespoon of yogurt.

Tip As the name suggests, hot smoked paprika is hotter than its milder counterpart and it adds a lovely smoky depth to this dish. If you're using standard sweet paprika, use 4 teaspoons.

Sweet, Sticky, Peppered Pork

A quick and easy recipe with vibrant flavours. Serve with 150 g (5½ oz) of cooked brown rice per person and a zero *ProPoints* value salad, adding 6 *ProPoints* values per serving.

Serves 4

2 tablespoons reduced sugar marmalade
4 x 150 g (5½ oz) pork escalopes
2 tablespoons peppercorns, crushed
calorie controlled cooking spray

For the sauce

2 tablespoons balsamic vinegar
150 ml (5 fl oz) orange juice
1 tablespoon wholegrain mustard
1 teaspoon cornflour

7 *ProPoints* values per serving
29 *ProPoints* values per recipe

260 calories per serving

Takes 25 minutes

✱ not recommended

1 Gently heat the marmalade in a pan with 2 tablespoons of water, then brush over the pork escalopes. Place the crushed peppercorns on a plate and press the escalopes down on to them so that the meat becomes covered with pepper.

2 Heat a non stick pan and spray with the cooking spray. Fry the escalopes in two batches for 2–3 minutes on each side until cooked through, then set aside and keep them warm while you make the sauce.

3 With the pan still on the heat, pour in the vinegar and scrape up all the leftover juices and bits left from the pork with a wooden spatula or spoon. Pour in the orange juice and stir in the mustard. Blend the cornflour with a tablespoon of water, add to the pan and bring to the boil. Boil for 1 minute, stirring, until the sauce has thickened.

4 Serve the pork with the sauce poured over.

Tip For a more attractive dish, buy mixed peppercorns, which include red, white and black ones.

Baked Cheesy Leeks

This dish is best made with young tender leeks at the start of the season, which is early autumn.

Serves 4

calorie controlled cooking spray

12 small leeks, trimmed and slit in half from top to bottom, then washed

4 eggs

200 g (7 oz) low fat soft cheese

200 g (7 oz) low fat natural yogurt

50 g (1¾ oz) rye crispbreads

salt and freshly ground black pepper

a few sprigs of fresh thyme, chopped, to serve (optional)

5 *ProPoints* values per serving
21 *ProPoints* values per recipe

254 calories per serving

Takes **20 minutes** to prepare,
40 minutes to cook

V

✳ not recommended

1 Preheat the oven to Gas Mark 4/180°C/fan oven 160°C. Spray a shallow ovenproof dish with the cooking spray. Bring a pan of water to the boil, add the leeks and blanch for 6–8 minutes, until just tender. Drain and arrange them in the ovenproof casserole dish.

2 Meanwhile, beat the eggs with the soft cheese and yogurt and some seasoning. Break up the crispbreads by putting them in a plastic bag and pounding them with a rolling pin, or do this in a food processor. Pour the cheese sauce over the leeks and scatter with the crispbread crumbs.

3 Bake for 35–40 minutes, until the top is crisp and brown and the sauce is bubbling. Serve scattered with the thyme, if using.

Store cupboard ideas Rye crispbreads are a good low *ProPoints* value alternative to bread. Use them in your lunch box with sandwich ingredients, or experiment with more creative ideas – such as replacing breadcrumb bases with the crisp base. Each rye crispbread has a *ProPoints* value of 1.

Mediterranean Turkey Rolls

Basil complements the turkey so well in these tasty rolls that the whole family will enjoy.

Serves 4

2 aubergines
2 red peppers
100 g (3½ oz) ricotta
a large bunch of fresh basil, chopped,
  with a few chopped leaves reserved
8 x 50 g (1¾ oz) thin turkey escalopes
calorie controlled cooking spray
1 garlic clove, crushed
2 tablespoons white wine vinegar
400 g can chopped tomatoes
1 teaspoon clear honey
salt and freshly ground black pepper

4 ProPoints values per serving
15 ProPoints values per recipe

205 calories per serving

Takes **45 minutes** + cooling

* not recommended

1 Preheat the oven to Gas Mark 6/200°C/fan oven 180°C. Place the whole aubergines and red peppers on a baking tray and bake for 20 minutes. Then leave to cool.

2 Meanwhile, put the ricotta in a bowl with half the chopped fresh basil and season. Season the turkey escalopes and then put them between two sheets of baking parchment, foil or cling film. Beat with a rolling pin or meat tenderising mallet until thin but not broken.

3 When the peppers are cool enough to handle, peel and de-seed them and then chop them finely. Mix with the ricotta and remaining basil. Put spoonfuls of this along one end of the turkey escalopes and then roll them up. Line a baking tray with foil and spray with the cooking spray. Place the rolls on the foil and bake in the oven for 10 minutes until golden and cooked through.

4 In the meantime, slice the aubergines in half lengthwise, scoop out all the flesh and chop well. Spray a frying pan with the cooking spray and sauté the garlic for 2 minutes, then add the white wine vinegar and the aubergine flesh.

5 Cook for 2 minutes, stirring, then add the tomatoes, seasoning, the reserved basil leaves and honey. Cook for 10 minutes. Check the seasoning and then serve poured over the turkey rolls.

Cooking basics How to choose an aubergine: aubergines can vary in colour, so this is not necessarily a good indicator. Look for firm, heavy aubergines that have no brown patches and a cleft at the wider end.

Tuscan Beans

A simple, aromatic garlic and herb bean dish that is great on its own or as an accompaniment to fish or meat; add the extra **ProPoints** values as necessary.

Serves 4

calorie controlled cooking spray
4 garlic cloves, crushed
2 x 400 g cans cannellini beans, drained and rinsed, or dried beans (see Cooking basics, below)
2 tablespoons olive oil
3 fresh sage leaves, chopped finely
juice of ½ a lemon
a small bunch of fresh parsley, chopped
salt and freshly ground black pepper

5 ProPoints values per serving
19 ProPoints values per recipe

170 calories per serving

Takes **15 minutes**

V

* not recommended

1 Heat a large non stick saucepan and spray with the cooking spray. Fry the garlic for 2 minutes until just softened, then add the beans, olive oil, sage and seasoning and toss together for a few minutes until heated through.

2 Add the lemon juice and parsley, stir and serve.

Cooking basics How to cook dried beans, such as borlotti, cannellini, flack, flageolet, kidney, butter, etc: To serve 4, place 200 g (7 oz) of dried beans in a large bowl, add enough water to cover the beans plus an extra couple of inches. Add a pinch of bicarbonate of soda and leave to soak overnight. Drain and rinse the beans, place in a saucepan and cover with water plus an extra couple of inches. Add half a peeled onion, 2–3 garlic cloves and a handful of mixed herbs (thyme, rosemary, sage, parsley, bay or coriander). Bring to the boil and boil vigorously for 10 minutes. Reduce the heat and simmer for between 50 minutes and 2 hours, topping up the water during cooking time if necessary. Add a teaspoon of salt towards the end of the cooking time (if it is added at the beginning it will cause the beans to remain tough). Cooking time will depend on the type and age of the beans; push the tip of a small knife into a bean to check for tenderness after about 50 minutes. When tender, drain, remove any vegetables and herbs and use the beans as required.

Summer Vegetable Casserole

Serve this bright and tasty stew with a generous portion of green beans or sugar snap peas for no extra *ProPoints* values.

Serves 4

calorie controlled cooking spray
2 onions, chopped
2 garlic cloves, crushed
2 small aubergines, cubed
2 large red peppers, de-seeded and diced
450 g (1 lb) potatoes, cubed
4 teaspoons fennel seeds, crushed
2 x 400 g cans chopped tomatoes
200 ml (7 fl oz) dry white wine
4 courgettes, sliced
salt and freshly ground black pepper

4 *ProPoints* values per serving
15 *ProPoints* values per recipe

246 calories per serving

Takes **45 minutes**

V

✳ not recommended

1 Heat a large lidded saucepan and spray with the cooking spray. Add the onions and garlic and stir fry for 2–3 minutes, until golden, adding a little water if necessary to prevent them from sticking.

2 Add the remaining ingredients, except the courgettes, and bring to the boil. Cover and simmer for 20 minutes, until the potatoes are cooked through.

3 Remove the lid, add the courgettes and simmer for a further 5 minutes until they are tender and the casserole is thick. Check the seasoning before serving.

> **Eat wisely** One of the most common causes of over eating is because the food is there. And the reason it is there is because it was picked up at the supermarket. Try to write out a shopping list for all the ingredients you require for your week; then make sure you're not hungry when you go shopping.

Mini Toad in the Hole

A fun way to serve up this family favourite; just add gravy (see Tip below) and your favourite zero *ProPoints* values vegetables.

Serves 4 (makes 12 puddings)

1 tablespoon sunflower oil
12 thin, low fat sausages
1 large onion, sliced
125 g (4½ oz) plain flour
1 egg
300 ml (10 fl oz) skimmed milk
salt and freshly ground black pepper

9 *ProPoints* values per serving
36 *ProPoints* values per recipe

114 calories per serving

Takes **15 minutes** to prepare,
20 minutes to cook

✳ not recommended

1 Preheat the oven to Gas Mark 7/220°C/fan oven 200°C. Divide the oil between the hollows in a 12 hole muffin tin (¼ teaspoon in each) and heat in the oven for 2 minutes.

2 Twist each of the sausages in half to form two cocktail sized sausages, and snip to separate.

3 Place two sausages and some onion in each hollow and cook in the oven for 8 minutes until lightly browned.

4 Meanwhile, sift the flour into a bowl and season. Make a well in the centre, break in the egg, and gradually whisk in the milk to give a smooth batter. Transfer to a jug.

5 When the sausages and onions are browned, pour in the batter, dividing it equally between the hollows. Return to the oven and cook for 18–20 minutes until the batters are risen, crisp and a rich golden brown. Serve three puddings per person.

Tip To make gravy, use 4 teaspoons of gravy granules made up with 250 ml (9 fl oz) of boiling water, for an extra 1 *ProPoints* value per serving.

Vegetarian variation For a vegetarian version, use eight medium vegetarian sausages, each cut into three chunks. Place two chunks in each hollow of the muffin tin and follow the rest of the method above. The *ProPoints* values will be 8 per serving.

Sizzled Chicken with Parsley Mash ⑨

This dish is ideal for the whole family, including children.

Serves 4

25 g (1 oz) plain flour

2 teaspoons dried sage

450 g (1 lb) skinless boneless chicken breasts, cut into chunks

1 tablespoon vegetable oil

2 garlic cloves, sliced finely

1 onion, sliced

2 apples, cored and chopped but unpeeled

150 ml (5 fl oz) hot chicken stock

150 ml (5 fl oz) unsweetened apple juice

125 g (4½ oz) mushrooms, sliced

700 g (1 lb 9 oz) potatoes, cut into chunks

4 tablespoons skimmed milk

2 tablespoons chopped fresh parsley, plus extra to garnish

salt and freshly ground black pepper

9 *ProPoints* values per serving
35 *ProPoints* values per recipe

400 calories per serving

Takes **30 minutes** to prepare, **25 minutes** to cook

✱ recommended

1 Sprinkle the flour and dried sage on to a plate and season. Roll the pieces of chicken in this mixture.

2 Heat the vegetable oil in a large, lidded, flameproof casserole or lidded saucepan and add the chicken, cooking over a medium heat until browned on all sides. Push to one side, then add the garlic, onion and apples and sauté for about 3 minutes.

3 Add the stock and apple juice, bring up to the boil, then cover and cook over a low heat for 20–25 minutes, adding the mushrooms after 15 minutes.

4 Meanwhile, bring a pan of water to the boil, add the potatoes and cook until tender. Mash well, adding the milk and parsley. Season to taste and serve with the chicken, garnished with extra chopped parsley.

Fish 'n' Chips

A low *ProPoints* value version of the traditional family favourite.

Serves 4

900 g (2 lb) potatoes
calorie controlled cooking spray
4 x 200 g (7 oz) skinless cod fillets
1 egg, beaten
100 g (3½ oz) fresh white breadcrumbs
lemon slices, to serve

10 *ProPoints* values per serving
42 *ProPoints* values per recipe

437 calories per serving

Takes **10 minutes** to prepare,
25 minutes to cook

* not recommended

1 Preheat the oven to Gas Mark 6/200°C/fan oven 180°C. Line two baking trays with non stick baking parchment.

2 Peel the potatoes and cut into chips. Place in a large container with a tight fitting lid and spray with the cooking spray. Place the lid on the container and shake thoroughly so the potatoes get coated with a thin film of the cooking spray. Arrange on a baking tray and cook for about 25 minutes.

3 Meanwhile, make sure there are no bones in the fish fillets. Dip the fish into the beaten egg and then into the breadcrumbs to coat evenly. Place on the other baking tray and spray with the cooking spray, turning them over so that both sides get coated.

4 Bake on the oven shelf below the chips for 20 minutes. Serve hot with the lemon slices and potato chips.

Tip Leave the skins on the potatoes if you wish.

Variation Serve with a tomato salsa. To make it, just de-seed and dice two ripe tomatoes. Mix with 1 teaspoon of chopped fresh herbs and 1 teaspoon of balsamic vinegar, for no additional *ProPoints* values.

Basque Chicken Casserole

Most of the cooking for this delicious dish is done in the oven without you having to worry about it.

Serves 4

calorie controlled cooking spray

4 x 175 g (6 oz) skinless boneless chicken breasts

225 g (8 oz) shallots, peeled but left whole

2 garlic cloves, crushed

400 g can chopped tomatoes

½ teaspoon paprika

2 red, yellow or orange peppers, de-seeded and chopped

2 bay leaves

150 ml (5 fl oz) dry white wine

salt and freshly ground black pepper

To serve

1 tablespoon capers

grated zest of a lemon

a small bunch of fresh basil, chopped

1 small red chilli, de-seeded and chopped finely (optional)

5 *ProPoints* values per serving
21 *ProPoints* values per recipe

265 **calories** per serving

Takes **25 minutes** to prepare,
1 hour to cook

✳ recommended

1 Preheat the oven to Gas Mark 2/150°C/fan oven 130°C. Heat a large non stick frying pan and spray with the cooking spray. Season the chicken breasts, then fry for 5–6 minutes until golden.

2 At the same time, in a large, lidded, flameproof casserole dish also on the hob, fry the shallots and garlic with the cooking spray for 4 minutes, until starting to brown. Add a little water if necessary to prevent them from sticking. Add the tomatoes, 100 ml (3½ fl oz) of water, the paprika, peppers, bay leaves, white wine and seasoning.

3 Bring to the boil. Add the chicken breasts, incorporating any juices from the base of the pan, and stir well. Cover and cook in the oven for 1 hour.

4 Remove from the oven, remove the bay leaves, check the seasoning and sprinkle with the capers, lemon zest, basil and chilli, if using, to serve.

Cooking basics How to make the most of red peppers: red peppers are not only delicious, but are also great in stir fries, risottos or roasted. They are also excellent stuffed and baked.

Chicken Tikka Masala

Serves 4

2 tablespoons tikka masala curry paste

150 g tub 0% fat Greek yogurt

450 g (1 lb) skinless boneless chicken breasts, cut into chunks

calorie controlled cooking spray

1 red onion, sliced thinly

1 teaspoon freshly grated root ginger or 1 teaspoon ready prepared 'fresh' ginger

400 g can chopped tomatoes

150 ml (5 fl oz) chicken stock

2 tablespoons chopped fresh coriander

100 g (3½ oz) dried basmati rice

salt and freshly ground black pepper

To garnish

5 cm (2 inch) cucumber, chopped finely

a few sprigs of fresh coriander

1 Put the curry paste into a non-metallic bowl and mix in the yogurt, reserving 60 g (2 oz) of it for later. Add the chicken, stir well and then cover and leave to marinate in the fridge for at least 1 hour or overnight.

2 When ready to cook, heat a large non stick saucepan and spray with the cooking spray. Add most of the onion, reserving some to garnish. Sauté for 1–2 minutes and then add the ginger and marinated chicken mixture. Cook for 2–3 minutes.

3 Add the tomatoes, stock and chopped coriander to the saucepan. Bring up to the boil, then reduce the heat and simmer, uncovered, over a low heat for 20–25 minutes. Season to taste.

4 When the chicken has simmered for 10 minutes, bring another pan of water to the boil, add the rice and cook according to the packet instructions.

5 Serve the rice with the cooked chicken, garnished with the reserved yogurt, remaining red onion, cucumber and coriander sprigs.

7 *ProPoints* values per serving
29 *ProPoints* values per recipe

274 **calories** per serving

Takes **15 minutes** to prepare + 1 hour marinating, **25 minutes** to cook

✳ recommended

Vegetarian variation Use the same quantity of Quorn pieces instead of the chicken for a vegetarian alternative. The *ProPoints* values per serving will remain the same.

Chicken and Spring Onion Burgers

Serves 4

500 g (1 lb 2 oz) chicken mince
6 spring onions, chopped finely
3 garlic cloves, crushed
2 tablespoons chopped fresh parsley
zest and juice of a lime
calorie controlled cooking spray
salt and freshly ground black pepper

To serve

4 medium burger buns
2 tablespoons tomato ketchup
salad leaves, tomato and cucumber

1 Mix together the mince, spring onions, garlic, parsley, lime zest and seasoning. Shape into four patties then heat a non stick frying pan and spray with the cooking spray. Fry the patties for 5–10 minutes on each side until cooked through.

2 Meanwhile, split the buns and toast lightly. Spread each half with ½ tablespoon of tomato ketchup then arrange the salad on the base of each bun and place a burger on top. Squeeze a little lime juice over, replace the top half of the bun and serve.

7 ProPoints values per serving
29 ProPoints values per recipe

270 calories per serving

Takes **20 minutes**

* not recommended

Tip Serve with 125 g (4½ oz) low fat oven chips per person, for an additional 4 **ProPoints** values per serving.

Variation Use the same amount of turkey mince instead of the chicken, for 8 **ProPoints** values per serving.

Easy Pizzas

Everyone loves pizza, and this low *ProPoints* values version provides a simple but satisfying meal.

Serves 2

calorie controlled cooking spray

1 small onion, chopped

200 g can chopped tomatoes with herbs

1 tablespoon tomato purée

23 cm (9 inch) thin and crispy pizza base weighing approx 100 g (3½ oz)

a choice of zero *ProPoints* value toppings (e.g. mushrooms, pepper strips, cherry tomatoes, lightly steamed broccoli florets, rocket, baby spinach, thin slices of red onion, capers, gherkins)

fresh herbs such as basil, parsley or oregano for the topping

salt and freshly ground black pepper

4 *ProPoints* values per serving
8 *ProPoints* values per recipe

C 275 **calories** per serving

Takes **40 minutes**

V

* recommended (freeze pizza bases and sauce separately)

1 To make the sauce, spray a small non stick saucepan with the cooking spray and fry the onion until soft, adding a little water if necessary to stop it from sticking. Add the tomatoes, tomato purée and seasoning.

2 Bring to the boil and then simmer on a low heat for 10–15 minutes, until thick. Turn off the heat and allow to cool. Preheat the oven to Gas Mark 7/220°C/fan oven 200°C.

3 Spoon the tomato sauce on to the pizza base and spread it out evenly to the edges.

4 Decorate the pizzas with the zero *ProPoints* value toppings of your choice and then bake for 15–20 minutes, until the edges are golden brown and the vegetables are charred. Scatter with the fresh herbs and serve.

Store cupboard ideas When you have an easy to multiply, freezeable recipe like these pizzas, try to make up two or three batches so you can freeze some for later. Divide into portions and freeze the extra batches you don't need so that you can just pull them out of the freezer and defrost them when you want.

Pancetta Pizza

Pancetta is Italian streaky bacon, usually smoked and often found diced for casseroles, pasta or, as here, pizzas.

Serves 4

calorie controlled cooking spray
144 g packet pizza base mix
130 g packet cubed pancetta
150 g (5½ oz) whole baby portobello or closed cap mushrooms, halved
1 red pepper, de-seeded and sliced
2 garlic cloves, sliced
5 tablespoons passata
2 tablespoons grated half fat Cheddar cheese

---

7 ProPoints values per serving
27 ProPoints values per recipe

281 calories per serving

Takes **25 minutes** to prepare,
20 minutes to cook

✳ not recommended

1 Preheat the oven to Gas Mark 7/220°C/fan oven 200°C. Spray a baking tray with the cooking spray. Mix the dough according to the packet instructions, making one large pizza about 20 cm (8 inches) in diameter.

2 Heat a large frying pan and dry fry the pancetta over a medium heat for 3–4 minutes until browned. Remove from the pan. Spray the pan with the cooking spray and heat until sizzling. Add the mushrooms and pepper and cook over a medium heat for 5 minutes. Add the garlic and cook for a further 2 minutes until the mushroom juices have evaporated. Remove from the heat.

3 Spread the passata over the pizza base, top with the mushroom mixture and cooked pancetta and sprinkle over the cheese. Bake for 15–20 minutes until golden and bubbling.

Tip Use four lean or extra lean back bacon rashers, cut into thin strips, if you can't find diced pancetta. The **ProPoints** values will be 4 per serving.

Variation Use two 165 g (5¾ oz) skinless boneless chicken breasts, cut into strips, instead of the pancetta. Spray the frying pan with the cooking spray and stir fry for 5 minutes until golden and cooked through. The **ProPoints** values will be reduced to 5 per serving.

Meatloaf

A contemporary version of this British classic. Serve hot with steamed zero *ProPoints* value vegetables or cold with a zero *ProPoints* value salad. The meatloaf will keep, covered, in the fridge for a few days.

Serves 4

calorie controlled cooking spray
250 g (9 oz) turkey mince
250 g (9 oz) fresh breadcrumbs
1 large onion, grated
2 courgettes, grated
2 carrots, peeled and grated
2 tablespoons tomato purée
1 egg, beaten
a small bunch of fresh sage or thyme, chopped, reserving a few sprigs or whole leaves for garnish
salt and freshly ground black pepper

6 *ProPoints* values per serving
25 *ProPoints* values per recipe

365 calories per serving

Takes **15 minutes** to prepare, **1 hour** to cook

recommended

1 Preheat the oven to Gas Mark 4/180°C/fan oven 160°C. Spray a 1 litre (1¾ pint) loaf tin with the cooking spray and then line with baking parchment.

2 Mix together all the remaining ingredients, except the herbs for the garnish, and pack into the tin. Cover with a piece of foil and bake for 1 hour or until the loaf begins to shrink away from the sides of the tin. Remove the foil for the last 15 minutes to brown the top.

3 Serve in slices, garnished with the reserved herbs.

Store cupboard ideas Tomato purée is a great product, which you should always try to keep in stock. It's made from concentrated tomatoes, adding a great tomato flavour to your dishes.

Savoury Tarte Tatin

The colourful topping of this upside down tart will begin to caramelise as it cooks, giving it a lovely thick glaze.

Serves 4

175 g (6 oz) courgettes, sliced
1 red onion, cut into thin wedges
225 g (8 oz) open cup mushrooms, halved
1 garlic clove, crushed
a sprig of fresh rosemary, chopped
1 tablespoon olive oil
1 teaspoon balsamic vinegar
175 g (6 oz) small tomatoes, halved
2 teaspoons plain white flour, for rolling
175 g (6 oz) puff pastry
salt and freshly ground black pepper

6 *ProPoints* values per serving
25 *ProPoints* values per recipe

C   245 calories per serving

Takes **30 minutes** to prepare,
20 minutes to cook

V

* recommended

1 Preheat the oven to Gas Mark 6/200°C/fan oven 180°C.

2 Mix together the courgettes, red onion, mushrooms, garlic, rosemary, olive oil, balsamic vinegar and seasoning. Arrange them on a non stick baking tray lined with baking parchment and roast for 15 minutes.

3 Remove the vegetables from the oven. Arrange all the vegetables, including the tomatoes, on the base of a 20 cm (8 inch) ovenproof non stick frying pan or cake tin.

4 Roll out the pastry on a lightly floured surface to make a 23 cm (9 inch) circle. Lay the pastry over the vegetables, tucking in the edges all the way round. Bake the tart in the oven for 20 minutes until the pastry is well risen and golden.

5 Carefully run a round bladed knife around the edge of the pan or tin. Put a large plate over the top and turn the pan or tin upside down, so the tart drops on to the plate. Cut the tart into quarters to serve.

Tip Make sure that if you are using a frying pan for this recipe it has a metal or ovenproof handle, otherwise use a round cake tin.

Variations Use other vegetables, such as de-seeded and diced red or green peppers or cubes of aubergine, in place of any of those used here.

Quorn Fajitas

A great tasting vegetarian version of this Mexican favourite.

Serves 4

2 tablespoons tomato ketchup
2 tablespoons dark soy sauce
2 garlic cloves, crushed
1 teaspoon chilli flakes
3 x 100 g (3½ oz) Quorn fillets, cut into
  long strips
calorie controlled cooking spray
225 g (8 oz) courgettes, sliced
2 red onions, cut into thin wedges
1 red pepper, de-seeded and sliced
8 flour tortillas
4 tablespoons low fat natural yogurt
2 tablespoons chopped fresh coriander
½ Iceberg lettuce, shredded, to garnish

10 *ProPoints* values per serving
38 *ProPoints* values per recipe

400 calories per serving

Takes **25 minutes**

V

✱   not recommended

1 In a bowl, mix together the tomato ketchup, soy sauce, garlic and chilli flakes. Add the Quorn and mix well.

2 Preheat the oven to Gas Mark 7/220°C/fan oven 200°C.

3 Spray a griddle pan or non stick frying pan with the cooking spray and heat it until it just starts smoking. Add the Quorn strips, courgettes, onions and pepper to the pan. Cook them for 5–6 minutes over a high heat, until everything is piping hot and beginning to char around the edges.

4 Wrap the tortillas in foil and heat them in the oven for 5 minutes.

5 Divide the filling between the eight tortillas, drizzle over a little yogurt, scatter on the coriander and roll them up tightly. Serve the fajitas with a garnish of shredded Iceberg lettuce, allowing two per serving.

Tip The tortillas can also be warmed in the microwave set on High. Depending on the power of your microwave, they will take roughly 30 seconds each – but don't wrap them in foil.

Turkey and Mushroom Potato Topped Pie

Serves 4

calorie controlled cooking spray
1 large onion, chopped
3 rashers lean back bacon
500 g (1 lb 2 oz) turkey breast meat, cut into
  bite size pieces
275 g (9½ oz) mushrooms, sliced thickly
300 ml (10 fl oz) chicken stock
5 or 6 sprigs of fresh thyme
900 g (2 lb) potatoes, peeled and chopped
2 leeks, sliced
100 g (3½ oz) low fat natural fromage frais
3 tablespoons skimmed milk
salt and freshly ground black pepper

9 ProPoints values per serving
37 ProPoints values per recipe

396 calories per serving

Takes **40 minutes** to prepare,
15 minutes to cook

* not recommended

1 Preheat the oven to Gas Mark 6/200°C/fan oven 180°C. Heat a large non stick pan, spray with the cooking spray and cook the onion and bacon for 3–4 minutes. Add the turkey and cook for 5–6 minutes before adding the mushrooms, stock, thyme and seasoning. Simmer for 15 minutes.

2 Meanwhile, bring a pan of water to the boil, add the potatoes and cook until tender. Spray a non stick frying pan with the cooking spray and fry the leeks.

3 When the turkey is cooked, stir in the fromage frais and, using a slotted spoon, spoon the mixture into an ovenproof dish. Pour in half of the liquid, discarding the rest.

4 Mash the potatoes with the skimmed milk and then, using a fork, stir in the leeks. Season well.

5 Top the turkey mixture with the potatoes and leeks and place in the oven for 15 minutes.

Cooking basics To clean mushrooms: in order to retain the full flavour of the mushrooms, clean them by gently wiping them with a clean, damp cloth rather than washing them. Dry them with a paper towel.

Delicious Desserts

Not everyone has a sweet tooth, but most grown ups – and children – like something 'for afters'. This chapter includes popular puddings and family favourites, including Roly Pavlova, Strawberry and Hazelnut Strata and Quick Fruit Crumble. Try new recipes too – everyone is sure to love home made ice creams such as Montezuma Ice Cream with Marshmallows.

Enjoy these delicious low fat versions of family favourites

Montezuma Ice Cream with Marshmallows

Montezuma was an Aztec king who was reported to have drunk vast quantities of a rich, dark, spiced hot chocolate every day.

Serves 6

2 x 22 g sachets instant, low fat, dark hot chocolate powder
4 tablespoons boiling water
500 g (1 lb 2 oz) 0% fat Greek yogurt
50 g (1¾ oz) plain chocolate (preferably 70% cocoa solids), melted
a pinch of allspice
a pinch of ground ginger
1 tablespoon honey
100 g (3½ oz) mini marshmallows

5 *ProPoints* values per serving
31 *ProPoints* values per recipe

C   175 calories per serving

Takes **10 minutes** + freezing

V

*   recommended

1 Mix the hot chocolate to a paste with the boiling water and place in a large bowl with all the remaining ingredients, except the marshmallows. Blend until smooth and evenly mixed. Fold in the marshmallows and then tip the mixture into a freezer container or ice cream maker and freeze.

2 If not using an ice cream maker, remove the ice cream from the freezer every hour and mash with a fork to break up the ice crystals.

3 Remove the ice cream from the freezer 30 minutes before you want to serve it, to allow it to soften.

Eat wisely If you enjoy your chocolate hit, use high cocoa content chocolate (70% or more) in your cooking. This way you'll still get the same strong chocolate taste, but you use less.

Home Made Vanilla Ice Cream

A delicious, velvety smooth ice cream for an irresistible, low *ProPoints* values treat.

Serves 6

600 ml (20 fl oz) skimmed milk
1 vanilla pod, split
2 egg yolks
25 g (1 oz) caster sugar
25 g (1 oz) cornflour
150 ml (5 fl oz) 0% fat Greek yogurt

3 *ProPoints* values per serving
16 *ProPoints* values per recipe

C 115 calories per serving

Takes **35 minutes** + **30 minutes** cooling + freezing + **20 minutes** standing

V

* recommended

1 Heat the milk and vanilla pod in a medium pan until the milk is just boiling. Remove the pan from the heat and whisk in the egg yolks and caster sugar.

2 Using a sieve, strain the mixture into a clean, medium non stick saucepan. Mix the cornflour with a little cold water to make a thin paste and add this to the pan. Cook, stirring continuously, until the custard mixture thickens. Cool, remove the vanilla pod and then chill for 30 minutes.

3 Pour the mixture and yogurt into an ice cream maker, if using, and churn for 20–25 minutes, or according to the manufacturer's instructions. Spoon into a plastic lidded container and place in the freezer for around 4 hours. (If you don't have an ice cream maker, whisk the yogurt into the chilled custard transfer it to a freezer container and freeze. After 2 hours remove it from the freezer and whisk well. Freeze for another 2 hours and then whisk again. Return it to the freezer until the ice cream is frozen solid.)

4 About 20 minutes before serving, take the ice cream out of the freezer and let it stand before scooping it out.

Tip When cooling custards, cover with a sheet of dampened greaseproof paper. This will prevent a skin from forming.

Cheesecake Ice Cream

Try this delicious creamy dessert for a special family dinner.

Serves 6

250 ml (9 fl oz) skimmed milk, chilled
100 g (3½ oz) low fat soft cheese
85 g (3 oz) caster sugar
finely grated zest and juice of 2 lemons

2 ProPoints values per serving
14 ProPoints values per recipe

88 calories per serving

Takes **10 minutes** to prepare + freezing
+ **20 minutes** standing

V

∗ recommended

1 Put all the ingredients into a food processor or liquidiser and whisk or blend until thoroughly blended. (You could also do this with an electric whisk.)

2 Pour the mixture into an ice cream maker, if using, and churn for 20–25 minutes, or according to the manufacturer's instructions. Spoon into a plastic lidded container and place in the freezer for around 4 hours. (If you don't have an ice cream maker, pour the whisked mixture into a lidded plastic container and freeze for 1½ hours. Remove from the freezer and stir it through with a fork to remove any lumps. Return it to the freezer for another 1½ hours, then repeat the stirring. Return it to the freezer and leave it for at least 8 hours or preferably overnight.)

3 If using an ice cream maker it will be ready to serve after 4 hours. (If not using an ice cream maker, or if not using immediately, remove from the freezer and leave to soften at room temperature for about 20 minutes before serving.)

Roly Pavlova

This is a delicious and refreshing dessert the whole family will love.

Serves 8

1 teaspoon vanilla essence
1 teaspoon vinegar
1 teaspoon cornflour
4 egg whites
200 g (7 oz) caster sugar
200 ml (7 fl oz) half fat crème fraîche
500 g (1 lb 2 oz) frozen summer fruits,
  defrosted and drained

4 *ProPoints* values per serving
33 *ProPoints* values per recipe

C 170 calories per serving

Takes **20 minutes** to prepare, **45 minutes** to cook + cooling

V

* not recommended

1 Preheat the oven to Gas Mark 2/150°C/fan oven 130°C. Line a 23 x 33 cm (9 x 13 inch) Swiss roll tin with baking parchment.

2 Blend together the vanilla essence, vinegar and cornflour.

3 In a separate grease-free bowl, using a hand held electric mixer, whisk the egg whites until they form stiff peaks. Whisk in the caster sugar and cornflour mixture in three equal quantities and continue whisking until the mixture is thick and glossy.

4 Spoon the meringue into the prepared tin and level the surface. Bake in the oven for 45 minutes, then turn off the oven. Leave the meringue in the cooling oven for 15 minutes.

5 Turn the meringue out on to a large sheet of greaseproof paper and carefully peel off the baking parchment. Allow to cool completely.

6 Spread the crème fraîche over the meringue and sprinkle with the fruit. Gently roll up from the narrow end, then serve.

Tip Do not worry if the meringue cracks when you roll it up; it adds to its charm.

Variation When soft summer fruits are in season, use them instead of frozen summer berries. Reserve a few for decoration.

Banoffee Pie

A deliciously indulgent low *ProPoints* values dessert.

Serves 6

40 g (1½ oz) low fat spread

135 g (4¾ oz) reduced fat digestive biscuits, crushed

calorie controlled cooking spray

1 sachet Angel Delight Butterscotch No Added Sugar

300 ml (10 fl oz) semi skimmed milk

2 bananas, chopped

200 g (7 oz) low fat natural yogurt

3 teaspoons muscovado sugar

---

6 *ProPoints* values per serving
36 *ProPoints* values per recipe

C **288 calories** per serving

Takes **15 minutes** + **30 minutes** chilling

V

✱ not recommended

1 Melt the low fat spread in a small saucepan. Add the crushed biscuits and mix well.

2 Spray a 20 cm (8 inch) loose bottomed flan tin with the cooking spray. Pour the crumb mixture into the tin and press it down well, right up to the edges.

3 Leave the flan tin in the fridge for 30 minutes.

4 Make up the butterscotch Angel Delight with the milk according to the sachet instructions. After leaving for 2 minutes, spoon it over the biscuit base and return it to the fridge for 4 minutes or until set.

5 Top with the chopped bananas and then the yogurt.

6 Sprinkle with the muscovado sugar and return to the fridge for 2 minutes until the sugar starts to dissolve. Serve the pie cut into six wedges.

Tip The biscuit base can be made well in advance and then you can complete the dessert just before you require it.

Variation Try using different flavours of Angel Delight with different fruits – try strawberry flavour, topped with 150 g (5½ oz) of fresh sliced strawberries, for the same *ProPoints* values.

Raspberry Orange Creams

These little desserts are like mini cheesecakes. Serve them with fresh raspberries and an orange and raspberry sauce.

Serves 4

350 g (12 oz) low fat soft cheese
4 tablespoons low fat natural yogurt
1 tablespoon caster sugar
finely grated zest of a lemon
1 tablespoon lemon juice
350 g (12 oz) raspberries
zest and juice of a large orange
artificial sweetener, to taste

1 Put the soft cheese into a bowl and beat with a wooden spoon to soften it. Add the yogurt, caster sugar, lemon zest and lemon juice.

2 Put four individual heart-shaped moulds with drainage holes on to a baking tray (or use yogurt pots with a couple of holes punched in the base). Spoon the cheese mixture into them, then cover and refrigerate for several hours, or overnight.

3 Reserve half the raspberries, then purée the other half in a blender or liquidiser with the orange juice. Sweeten to taste with the sweetener.

4 Turn out the desserts and serve with the reserved raspberries and the orange and raspberry sauce. Decorate with orange zest.

4 *ProPoints* values per serving
15 *ProPoints* values per recipe

C **180 calories** per serving

Takes **10 minutes** + several hours chilling

V

✳ not recommended

Tip If you line the pots with dampened butter muslin or new J-cloths (cut to size), you will be able to turn out the desserts easily.

Variation You can serve the desserts in their pots, if you prefer. Just top with the sauce and raspberries, then decorate with orange zest.

Blackberry Meringue Pudding

Here, little pots of blackberries are cooked with cinnamon and mallow meringue. An easy recipe for two or simply scale the ingredients up for more servings.

Serves 4

30 g (1¼ oz) fresh breadcrumbs
1 teaspoon ground cinnamon
220 g (7½ oz) fresh blackberries
2 egg whites
80 g (3 oz) light muscovado or soft brown sugar

1 Preheat the oven to Gas Mark 5/190°C/fan oven 170°C.

2 Heat a small non stick frying pan over a low heat and dry fry the breadcrumbs and cinnamon, stirring occasionally, until toasted and crisp. Remove from the heat and fold through the blackberries.

3 In a small, grease-free bowl, whisk the egg white to stiff peaks. Whisk in half the sugar and then fold in the remainder. Fold the blackberry mixture through the meringue and divide between four 8 cm (3¼ inch) ramekin dishes. Bake for 15 minutes until golden.

3 *ProPoints* values per serving
11 *ProPoints* values per recipe

C **116 calories** per serving

Takes **10 minutes** to prepare,
15 minutes to cook

V

* not recommended

Variation Replace some of the blackberries with redcurrants or blueberries, or all the fruits with fresh raspberries. The ***ProPoints*** values will remain the same.

Quick Fruit Crumble

This simple and satisfying dessert is assembled in no time at all using a can of fruit and a quickly whizzed up crumble topping – just right for a midweek pudding. Serve with 1 tablespoon of low fat natural yogurt, for an extra 1 *ProPoints* value per serving.

Serves 4

420 g can peaches in natural juice, drained
1 ripe banana, sliced thinly
50 g (1¾ oz) low fat spread
100 g (3½ oz) plain white flour
1 tablespoon light soft brown sugar
2 tablespoons porridge oats
freshly grated nutmeg

5 *ProPoints* values per serving
20 *ProPoints* values per recipe

C   **240 calories** per serving

Takes **10 minutes** to prepare,
20 minutes to cook

V

✱   not recommended

1   Preheat the oven to Gas Mark 5/190°C/fan oven 170°C.

2   Tip the canned peaches into a medium baking dish – chop them if necessary. Mix in the banana slices.

3   Place the low fat spread, flour and sugar in a food processor and whizz until the mixture resembles fine breadcrumbs. Stir in the porridge oats. Spoon this topping over the fruit and sprinkle over nutmeg.

4   Place the dish on a baking tray and bake in the oven for 20 minutes until the topping is lightly browned.

Rhubarb Crumble

Serve this old favourite hot with 1 tablespoon of virtually fat free fromage frais, for an extra 1 *ProPoints* value per serving.

Serves 6

1 kg (2 lb 4 oz) rhubarb, trimmed and cut into small pieces
3 tablespoons artificial sweetener
100 g (3½ oz) plain white or wholemeal flour
100 g (3½ oz) porridge oats
50 g (1¾ oz) demerara sugar
1 teaspoon ground cinnamon
50 g (1¾ oz) low fat spread, straight from the fridge

1 Preheat the oven to Gas Mark 6/200°C/fan oven 180°C. Place the rhubarb in a saucepan with 200 ml (7 fl oz) of water and the sweetener. Cover and simmer for 10 minutes until soft then pour into a 1.2 litre (2 pint) ovenproof dish.

2 Put the flour, oats, demerara sugar and cinnamon in a food processor. Cut the low fat spread into pieces and add to the dry mixture. Pulse to make a coarse blend.

3 Sprinkle the crumble mixture over the rhubarb and bake for 20–30 minutes, until pale golden and the fruit bubbles up at the edges.

5 *ProPoints* values per serving
31 *ProPoints* values per recipe

193 calories per serving

Takes **10 minutes** to prepare, **30 minutes** to bake

V

✻ not recommended

Variation This could also be made with canned rhubarb or with fresh gooseberries, apricots, plums, apples or pears.

Cherry and Almond Omelette

Cherries and almonds conjure up memories of Italy with its lovely fruit orchards.

Serves 6

25 g (1 oz) butter
2 x 425 g cans pitted black cherries in natural juice, drained
4 eggs, beaten
100 g (3½ oz) low fat natural fromage frais
25 g (1 oz) caster sugar
25 g (1 oz) ground almonds
15 g (½ oz) flaked almonds
icing sugar, for dusting

1 Melt the butter in a large heavy based frying pan. (The handle needs to be able to withstand the heat of the grill). Heat the cherries in the butter for 3–4 minutes or until slightly softened.

2 Beat together the eggs, fromage frais, sugar and ground almonds. Pour over the cherries. Stir for 3–4 minutes, then leave to lightly set for a further 5 minutes. Preheat the grill to medium.

3 Sprinkle the flaked almonds over the top and place under the grill to lightly toast the nuts. Serve warm, dusted with icing sugar.

4 *ProPoints* values per serving
24 *ProPoints* values per recipe

C **230 calories** per serving

Takes **25 minutes**

V

✳ not recommended

Variation Serve with a 60 g (2 oz) scoop of low fat vanilla ice cream, for an extra 2 *ProPoints* values per serving.

Apple Pie

Always a favourite with family and friends, this apple pie is packed with flavour and is delicious served hot or cold.

Serves 6

calorie controlled cooking spray
700 g (1 lb 9 oz) cooking apples, peeled,
 cored and quartered
2 tablespoons honey
50 g (1¾ oz) caster sugar
1 tablespoon cornflour
2 teaspoons cinnamon
zest and juice of a lemon
½ teaspoon vanilla essence

For the pastry

75 g (2¾ oz) plain flour, seasoned with
 ½ teaspoon salt
50 g (1¾ oz) low fat spread
a little skimmed milk, to glaze

---

4 *ProPoints* values per serving
24 *ProPoints* values per recipe

C 176 calories per serving

Takes **25 minutes** to prepare + cooling,
30 minutes to cook

V

* recommended

1 Preheat the oven to Gas Mark 5/190°C/fan oven 170°C and spray a 20 cm (8 inch) pie dish with the cooking spray.

2 Make the pastry by mixing together 1 tablespoon of the flour, the low fat spread and 2 teaspoons of water with a fork. Then add the rest of the flour and mix together. Turn out on to a floured board and knead lightly just until it comes together into a ball. Put in a plastic bag and refrigerate until needed.

3 Put the apples in a lidded pan with 4 tablespoons of water, cover and simmer gently for 10 minutes until the apples are beginning to soften. Add the honey, sugar, cornflour, cinnamon, lemon zest and juice and vanilla and stir until thick. Leave to cool slightly.

4 Roll out the pastry to fit the top of the dish with a little to spare. Put the apple in the dish and cover with the pastry. Press the edges down on top of the sides of the dish and cut off any excess. Make short slashes in the centre with a knife to allow the steam to escape and decorate with the pastry trimmings cut into leaf shapes.

5 Brush the pastry with a little skimmed milk and bake for 30 minutes or until the pastry is golden and crisp.

Lemon Meringue Pie

This is a simply delicious low *ProPoints* values version of the traditional favourite.

Serves 4

For the pastry
150 g (5½ oz) plain flour
a pinch of salt
75 g (2¾ oz) low fat spread

For the filling
3 tablespoons cornflour
150 ml (5 fl oz) water
grated zest and juice of 2 lemons
50 g (1¾ oz) caster sugar

For the meringue
2 egg whites
50 g (1¾ oz) caster sugar

10 *ProPoints* values per serving
40 *ProPoints* values per recipe

C 341 **calories** per serving

Takes **30 minutes** to prepare +
30 minutes chilling, **30 minutes** to cook

V

* recommended (base only)

1 To make the pastry, mix the flour and salt together. Rub in the low fat spread until the mixture resembles breadcrumbs.

2 Sprinkle over 1–2 tablespoons of water and mix with a palette knife until the pastry comes together into lumps. Draw it together quickly with your hand, wrap in cling film and place in the refrigerator for at least 30 minutes.

3 Preheat the oven to Gas Mark 7/220°C/fan oven 200°C. On a floured surface, roll out the dough to fit a shallow 20 cm (8 inch) tart tin. Prick all over with a fork and line with foil or baking parchment and scatter with baking beans (ordinary dried beans will do). Bake for 15 minutes.

4 Remove the beans and foil or parchment and bake for a further 5 minutes.

5 Mix the cornflour with the water in a saucepan. Add the lemon zest and juice and bring to the boil, stirring, until the mixture thickens. Add the sugar and stir.

6 Pour the filling into the pastry case and make the meringue. In a clean, grease-free bowl, whisk the egg whites until they form stiff peaks, then whisk in half the sugar. Fold in the rest of the sugar and then pile the meringue on top of the lemon mixture.

7 Bake for 10 minutes or until the meringue is crisp and lightly browned. Leave to cool before serving or the centre will be runny.

Variation For key lime pie, follow the same recipe but use limes instead of the lemons.

Lemon and Ginger Tart

This is a soft-setting tart, rather than a firmly set one like a cheesecake. Try it, it is absolutely delicious.

Serves 6

25 g (1 oz) low fat spread
10 reduced fat ginger snap biscuits, crushed
2 large lemons, preferably unwaxed
405 g can skimmed light condensed milk

8 *ProPoints* values per serving
47 *ProPoints* values per recipe

281 calories per serving

Takes **15 minutes** + chilling

V

* not recommended

1 Melt the low fat spread in a pan over a low heat. Add the crushed ginger snaps and 1 tablespoon of water and mix well. Press into a 20 cm (8 inch) pie dish. Chill until required.

2 Finely grate the zest of both lemons. Squeeze the juice from one lemon and half of the other, reserving the remaining half lemon to slice. Mix the juice into the condensed milk, which will thicken almost immediately, and then spoon over the biscuit base. Smooth the surface and chill for at least 1 hour until softly set.

3 Thinly slice the remaining lemon and use to decorate the tart.

Eat wisely Subtle changes in your usual eating habits can make a big difference to the way that you feel. Make gradual adjustments like reducing the amount of processed foods you eat.

Hot Chocolate Cake

Indulge your passion for chocolate with this delicious recipe that the whole family will love.

Serves 4

55 g (2 oz) low fat spread
55 g (2 oz) caster sugar
1 egg
40 g (1½ oz) self raising flour
15 g (½ oz) cocoa powder

5 ProPoints values per serving
19 ProPoints values per recipe

C   **170 calories** per serving

Takes **10 minutes**

V

*   recommended

1   Cream together the low fat spread and sugar in a 1.2 litre (2 pint) pudding basin.

2   Beat in the egg and then carefully fold in the flour and cocoa powder.

3   Mix well and then microwave on High for 2 minutes.

4   Allow to stand for 3–4 minutes, then turn out and serve immediately.

Cooking basics Eggs are versatile, and indispensable in the kitchen. Always bring eggs up to room temperature before using, as a cold egg won't whisk well and the shell will crack if placed in hot water.

Black Forest Trifle Cake

This recipe is a bit of a cross between a tiramisu and a Black Forest gâteau. Needless to say, it is utterly delicious but it is also very quick and easy to make, too.

Serves 6

24 sponge fingers
2 x 400 g cans stoned cherries in natural juice, drained, 6 tablespoons of juice reserved
2 tablespoons kirsch or brandy (optional)
200 g (7 oz) very low fat fromage frais
150 g (5½ oz) Quark
50 g (1¾ oz) icing sugar
1 teaspoon vanilla essence
1 teaspoon cocoa powder, for dusting

5 *ProPoints* values per serving
28 *ProPoints* values per recipe

259 calories per serving

Takes **25 minutes** to prepare
+ **30 minutes** chilling

V

✳ not recommended

1 Line the base and sides of a 900 g (2 lb) loaf tin with cling film, allowing extra to hang over the sides. Place a layer of eight sponge fingers in the bottom, sugar side down, and then arrange half the cherries on top and sprinkle with half the reserved cherry juice and 1 tablespoon of the kirsch or brandy, if using.

2 Beat half of the fromage frais with the Quark, sugar and vanilla essence until smooth. Spread half of this mixture over the cherries. Then arrange another layer of sponge fingers on top. Repeat with the remaining cherries, juice, kirsch or brandy and cheese mixture, finishing with a layer of sponge fingers.

3 Fold the cling film over the top and press down with your fingers; then chill for at least 30 minutes.

4 Turn out on to a serving plate and remove the cling film. Spread the top with the remaining fromage frais and dust with the cocoa powder.

Summer Puddings

In these individual summer puddings, the bread is layered in small pudding basins to make them easy to assemble – and they look so attractive when turned out.

Serves 2

75 g (2¾ oz) redcurrants or blackcurrants
75 g (2¾ oz) blueberries
1 tablespoon caster sugar
75 g (2¾ oz) strawberries, sliced
75 g (2¾ oz) raspberries
3 medium slices white bread

To serve

2 tablespoons very low fat natural
  fromage frais
a few mint leaves

5 *ProPoints* values per serving
9 *ProPoints* values per recipe

C   190 calories per serving

Takes **20 minutes**
+ several hours chilling

V

✱   recommended

1 Reserve two sprigs of redcurrants or blackcurrants and put the remainder in a medium saucepan with the blueberries and sugar. Heat gently until the juice just begins to run – about 2–3 minutes. Remove from the heat and stir in the strawberries and raspberries. Leave to cool.

2 Use biscuit cutters to stamp out circles from the slices of bread to fit into two individual pudding basins. You will need two 5 cm (2 inch) circles, two 6 cm (2½ inch) circles and two 7.5 cm (2¾ inch) circles.

3 Pop the smallest bread circles in the base of each pudding basin. Using a draining spoon (slotted spoon), divide half the fruit mixture between the basins. Place a medium-sized bread circle on top of each and then spoon in the rest of the fruit, reserving some of the juice. Finish with the largest circles of bread, pressing each down well.

4 Spoon a little remaining fruit juice over the bread and then place cling film tightly over. Place a weight on top of each basin. Refrigerate for several hours, or overnight if you prefer.

5 To serve, run a knife around the inside of each basin, and turn the puddings out on to individual plates. Serve each one with a tablespoon of fromage frais and decorate with the mint leaves and the reserved fruit sprigs.

Tips Whizz the leftover bread in a blender or food processor to make breadcrumbs, pack in a polythene bag and refrigerate or freeze to use in another recipe.

Try using defrosted frozen summer berries in this recipe – there's no need for any cooking, as they are already soft.

Chocolate Profiteroles

Discover the miracle of low *ProPoints* values profiteroles.

Serves 4 (Makes 12)

25 g (1 oz) low fat spread
75 g (2¾ oz) plain flour
a pinch of salt
1 egg
1 egg yolk
500 g tub 0% fat Greek yogurt
2 teaspoons vanilla essence
1 tablespoon clear honey
2 tablespoons cornflour
2 tablespoons low fat drinking chocolate
300 ml (10 fl oz) skimmed milk

8 *ProPoints* values per serving
31 *ProPoints* values per recipe

C **300 calories** per serving

Takes **25 minutes** to prepare, **20 minutes** to cook

V

* not recommended

1 Preheat the oven to Gas Mark 6/200°C/fan oven 180°C and line a baking tray with non stick baking parchment.

2 Heat the low fat spread and 150 ml (5 fl oz) of water together in a large saucepan until the spread has just melted. Meanwhile, put the flour on to a piece of baking parchment with the salt and mix together.

3 Take the saucepan off the heat and, working quickly, add all the flour mix into the pan using the baking parchment as a funnel. Beat together with a wooden spoon for at least 1 minute until well blended and the mixture comes away from the side of the pan in one lump.

4 Allow to cool for 10 minutes. Beat together the whole egg and the egg yolk and add to the cooled mixture, half at a time. Beat with a wooden spoon until the mixture is smooth, thick and glossy – this is quite hard. Place 12 heaped teaspoons well apart on the baking tray.

5 Bake for 15–20 minutes until well risen and golden. Remove from the oven and, with a sharp knife, slit each profiterole to let the air out. Place back in the turned off oven, the door slightly ajar so they dry out inside and cool.

6 Mix together the yogurt, vanilla and honey. Spoon into the cool profiteroles. Pile them up on a serving plate.

7 Blend the cornflour and drinking chocolate with a little of the milk in a saucepan. Blend in the rest of the milk, bring to the boil, stirring all the time, until thickened and smooth. Pour over the profiteroles to serve.

Bread and Peach Pudding

A unique and very tasty version of a much loved classic.

Serves 4

calorie controlled cooking spray
3 thick slices brown bread
410 g can peaches in natural juice
2 tablespoons mixed dried fruit
200 ml (7 fl oz) semi skimmed milk
2 eggs, beaten
½ teaspoon ground nutmeg
2 teaspoons muscovado sugar

5 *ProPoints* values per serving
19 *ProPoints* values per recipe

C 210 calories per serving

Takes **15 minutes** to prepare,
40 minutes to cook

V

✳ not recommended

1 Preheat the oven to Gas Mark 4/180°C/fan oven 160°C. Spray a medium, shallow, ovenproof dish with the cooking spray.

2 Break up the slices of bread and place them in the dish.

3 Drain the peaches, reserving the juice, and chop them roughly. Place them in the dish with the bread. Sprinkle over the mixed dried fruit.

4 Whisk together the reserved juice, milk and eggs and pour this over the bread and fruit.

5 Sprinkle the top with the nutmeg and muscovado sugar and bake in the oven for 40 minutes, until golden.

Variation Most fruits work well in this recipe – try tinned pears or apricots for a change. The *ProPoints* values will remain the same.

Rhubarb and Orange Fool

A fruit-flavoured fromage frais lends a lot more flavour to this easy dessert.

Serves 6

350 g (12 oz) rhubarb, trimmed and cut into chunks
finely grated zest and juice of an orange
50 g (1¾ oz) fructose
150 g (5½ oz) low fat ready-to-serve custard
11 g sachet gelatine
200 g tub orange flavour fromage frais
1 egg white

3 *ProPoints* values per serving
17 *ProPoints* values per recipe

80 calories per serving

Takes **20 minutes** + cooling
+ **2 hours** chilling

V

✳ not recommended

1 Place the rhubarb in a saucepan with the orange zest and juice and fructose. Cook over a gentle heat until the rhubarb is pulpy and then remove from the heat. Allow to cool.

2 When cool, transfer to a food processor with the custard and blend until smooth.

3 Place 3 tablespoons of water in a small heatproof dish and sprinkle the gelatine over. Allow to stand for 5 minutes, until it looks spongy, then heat gently over a pan of simmering water until the gelatine dissolves. Add to the food processor and blend for a couple of seconds.

4 Pour the rhubarb mixture into a mixing bowl and stir in the fromage frais. In a clean, grease-free bowl, whisk the egg white until it forms soft peaks and fold into the rhubarb mixture. Transfer to six individual glasses and chill for at least 2 hours before serving.

Tip You'll find fructose in the supermarket next to the sugar.

Variation Try using strawberry or peach flavoured fromage frais for a change, for the same *ProPoints* values.

Fruity Chocolate Fridge Cake

Serves 8

110 g (4 oz) plain chocolate (at least 70% cocoa solids)

50 g (1¾ oz) low fat spread

2 egg whites

125 g (4½ oz) low fat digestive biscuits, crushed roughly

75 g (2¾ oz) ready to eat dried apricots, chopped

---

5 ProPoints values per serving
41 ProPoints values per recipe

C **192 calories** per serving

Takes **15 minutes** + **2 hours** chilling

V

* not recommended

1 Place the chocolate and low fat spread in a heatproof bowl. Bring a small pan of water to simmer, rest the bowl over the pan and stir to melt. Alternatively, melt the chocolate and low fat spread in a microwave. Set aside to cool slightly.

2 Meanwhile, in a clean, grease-free bowl, whisk the egg whites until they form stiff peaks. Carefully fold the whites into the chocolate mixture followed by the biscuits and apricots, reserving a few of the chopped apricots to decorate the top.

3 Spread the mixture over the base of a loose bottomed 20 cm (8 inch) pie tin and decorate with the reserved apricots. Chill for at least 2 hours before cutting into wedges.

Chocolate Roulade

Serves 6

calorie controlled cooking spray
75 g (2¾ oz) plain white flour
2 tablespoons unsweetened cocoa powder
3 large eggs
75 g (2¾ oz) caster sugar
200 g (7 oz) low fat soft cheese
100 ml (3½ fl oz) very low fat raspberry
  fromage frais
100 g (3½ oz) raspberries, defrosted if frozen
2 teaspoons icing sugar, for dusting
a few mint leaves, to decorate

1 Preheat the oven to Gas Mark 7/220°C/fan oven 200°C. Spray a 18 x 28 cm (7 x 11 inch) Swiss roll tin with the cooking spray and line it with greaseproof paper. Spray the paper with the cooking spray.

2 Sift the flour and cocoa powder into a bowl. Set aside. Break the eggs into a large mixing bowl and add the caster sugar. Using a hand held electric mixer, whisk them together until very light and pale in colour. This will take about 5 minutes.

3 Sift the flour and cocoa mixture again, this time into the egg mixture. Fold it in gently using a large metal spoon, not a wooden one. Pour the mixture into the prepared tin and spread it out to the corners.

4 Bake in the oven for 7–9 minutes, until firm yet springy when you touch it. Turn it out on to a large sheet of greaseproof paper and then carefully peel away the lining paper. Cover with a clean, damp tea towel and leave the sponge until cold.

5 Mix together the soft cheese and fromage frais. Reserve a few raspberries for decoration, and then lightly mash the remainder with a fork. Stir these into the soft cheese mixture.

6 Trim the edges of the chocolate sponge, fill with the raspberry mixture and roll it up. Sprinkle with icing sugar and serve, decorated with the mint leaves and reserved raspberries.

6 *ProPoints* values per serving
34 *ProPoints* values per recipe

C **220 calories** per serving

Takes **30 minutes**

V

✳ recommended

Variation To make a peach melba roulade, omit the cocoa powder from the mixture, use a peach or raspberry flavoured fromage frais and add a chopped peach to the filling. The *ProPoints* values per serving will remain the same.

Strawberry and Hazelnut Strata

Serves 4

40 g (1½ oz) fresh breadcrumbs
25 g (1 oz) demerara sugar
15 g (½ oz) chopped hazelnuts
300 g (10½ oz) strawberries, sliced
1 tablespoon icing sugar
500 g (1 lb 2 oz) low fat custard, chilled

1 Preheat the oven to Gas Mark 4/180°C/fan oven 160°C.

2 Mix the breadcrumbs with the sugar and hazelnuts and spread out on a tray lined with baking parchment.

3 Bake for 8 minutes, stirring halfway through, until the crumbs are caramelised and crisp. Cool.

4 Mix the strawberries with the icing sugar to sweeten.

5 Layer the chilled custard, strawberries and crunchy hazelnut crumbs into four dessert glasses or bowls. Serve immediately.

5 *ProPoints* values per serving
19 *ProPoints* values per recipe

C **191 calories** per serving

Takes **10 minutes** to prepare, **8 minutes** to cook + cooling

V

* not recommended

Index